D1101545

The recipes in this cookbook are available on a companion Thermomix® Recipe Chip. Because we continuously check and update our recipes, there may be minor differences between the cookbook and the Thermomix® Recipe Chip. However, all recipes, whether newly updated or not, have been tested and are fully functional.

A Taste of India

Welcome

DEAR CUSTOMER,

We are very excited to present our new Indian cookbook.

Choosing a theme for our next cookbook was a simple decision for us. Indian food is immensely popular in Great Britain and Ireland today, and going out for a curry has become such a regularity that it is recognised as part of our culture.

Furthermore, our TM31 cookbook *Fast & Easy Indian Cooking* (Rosie Laljee & Janie Turner) was incredibly successful, so we knew we had to produce a TM5 cookbook that would be loved just as much. We have kept a handful of the most popular recipes from that first cookbook which provided the perfect starting point. *A Taste of India* is also available as a Recipe Chip, so you can use the Guided Cooking function on your TM5 – making Indian cooking even easier!

Indian food is as diverse as the people who eat it. There are the Indian dishes we make in our homes, those we eat in restaurants, and those served authentically in India and its subcontinents –and everything in between. Many of the most popular curries here today never originated in India at all. And of course every Indian restaurant or cook will have a different way of making the same dish. We have tried to create recipes that reflect the varied nature of Indian cuisine, but make it so much easier to recreate in your own home because you own a Thermomix®!

From simple starters, to rich, meaty curries, lighter fish dishes and plenty of vegetarian choices, there are many options for both easy midweek meals and more elaborate Indian banquets to impress your friends and family. We have also included some delicious sweet options to complete your meal. And if this book whets your appetite, you'll find even more Indian recipes on the Thermomix® Recipe Platform: www.mythermomix.co.uk.

We trust that we have included everyone's favourites in here, as well as providing inspiration with some new ideas. We hope you enjoy creating your own Indian feasts at home.

Happy Cooking,

Your Thermomix Team
UK and Ireland

Contents

INTRODUCTION

BASICS

STARTERS AND LIGHT MEALS

MAINS – MEAT

MAINS – FISH AND SEAFOOD

MAINS – VEGETARIAN

ON THE SIDE (PICKLES AND SALADS)

RICE AND BREADS

SWEET THINGS AND DRINKS

WHAT IS INDIAN FOOD?

India is a vast country with many languages, religions and cultures. Indian cuisine varies from region to region, according to the influence of settlers centuries ago, the raw fruits, vegetables and spices available, as well as the religion and traditions.

For instance, the cow is considered a sacred animal in India so beef would not feature in authentic Indian recipes. In addition, each family will have their own recipes, passed down through generations, all of which vary as tastes change.

As such, it is difficult to describe 'Indian food' as a whole, except to say that there are common threads that run through the dishes. Generally speaking, Indian food is spiced, fragrant and colourful.

It is a misconception that all Indian food is hot; while it is true that there are some spices which are warming and may contribute a little to the 'heat' in the dishes, by and large the spices give flavour and zing – and the chillies give heat. Most dishes would be uncompromised by reducing the chillies (in any form – powder, fresh or ground). If there is a particular spice you dislike you might leave it out, but it is preferable to use them in the proportions recommended as it is the medley of all the spices together that creates the best flavour.

Variations in taste and texture also play a part in Indian cooking according to when the spices are added in the cooking process, whether the dish is dry or wet, whether it has a tomato, nut or a cream base, and so on.

India is a country with diverse customs, some associated with how food is consumed. Meals are traditionally eaten whilst sitting on the floor, or on very low stools or cushions. Cutlery is rarely provided – instead the fingers of the right hand are used, and flatbreads are used to scoop up curry.

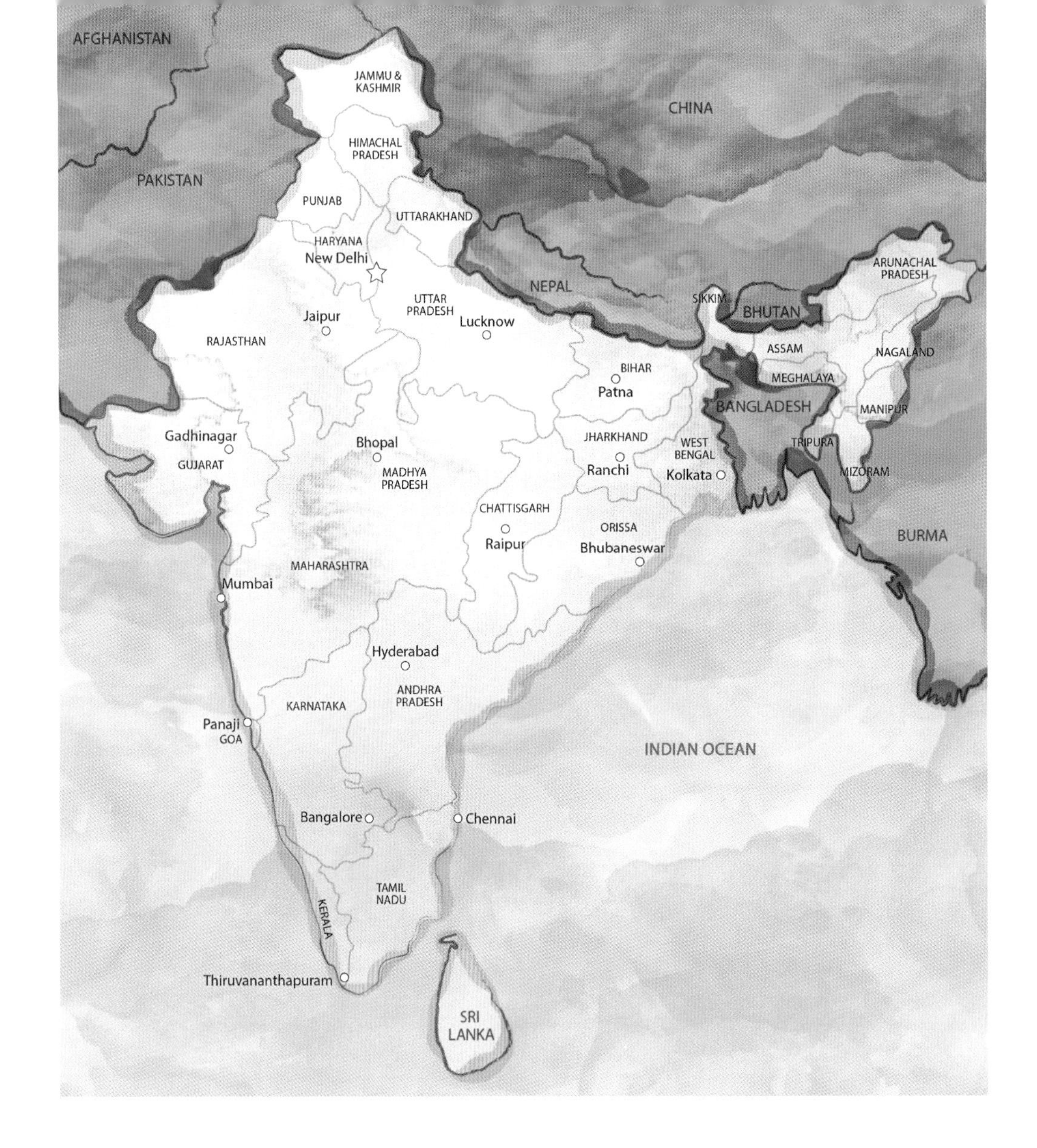

The word 'curry' is used more in the West than in India, and describes the sauce or gravy cooked with meat and/or vegetables. However, there is a vast array of food which has no gravy or sauce but is still very much Indian cuisine! In this book we have given you a cross-section of Indian food that has become popular in the UK and Ireland, but we have also introduced some less well-known dishes.

The Thermomix® works wonders to make Indian food easy and you should never have to buy another Indian ready meal or takeaway. With precise measurements, timings and directions you can enjoy a delicious banquet in your own home. We have not used any spices or other ingredients that are not easily available in the UK and Ireland. In some recipes we may have steered away from the traditional cooking method in order to simplify the process and save you time, however, we don't believe we have compromised on the end result.

Think of Indian cooking and an image of a huge array of different coloured spices is instantly conjured up. It is the selective use of these aromatic spices that make Indian cooking so unique. Some dishes will need only one or two spices to create their distinctive taste, and others will need a greater combination. Spices encompass seeds, pods, berries, bark, leaves and flower buds. Once harvested, the spice is dried to preserve it – either naturally by leaving it in the sun, or artificially. This encapsulates the oils for months, sometimes years. That oil is released by frying, toasting, roasting or boiling – which is why cooking Indian produces the most exquisite aroma!

But of course Indian cuisine isn't only about using whole spices. You'll find that a lot of recipes call for ground spices and this is where your Thermomix® really comes into play. Ground spice mixes, such as garam masala, are essential to curries and with a Thermomix® you're able to make your own homemade version with very little effort and in very little time. Not only that, but the flavour is so much fresher and far superior when you grind spices yourself. Many spices are too difficult for the home cook to grind – they're either too brittle, or the chillies too hot, as well as being very labour-intensive if you use a pestle and mortar. Thermomix® takes these problems out of your hands – and it's not just the grinding either; you can toast them in minutes too, all in the same bowl.

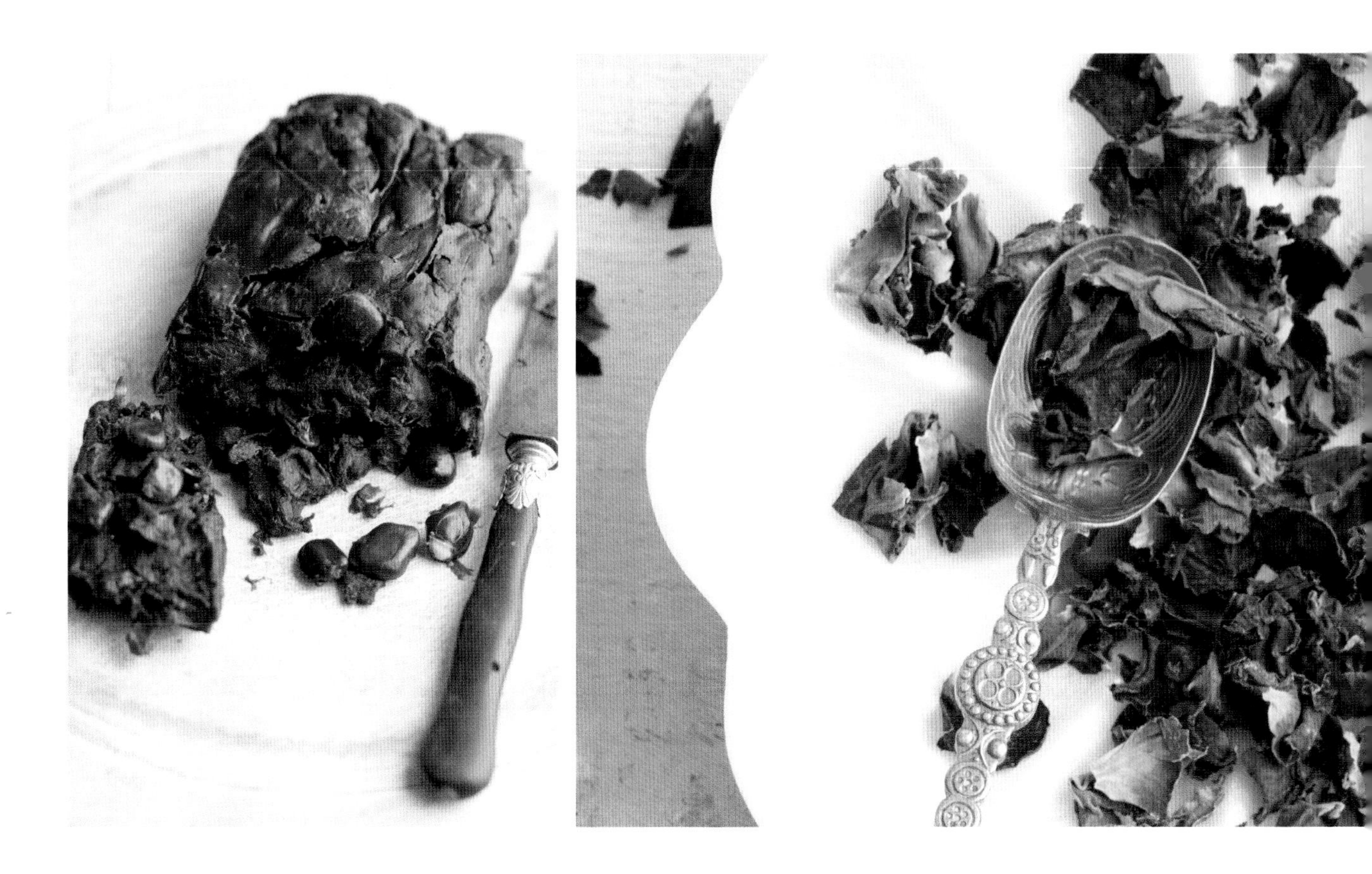

Of course it isn't just spices that Indian cooking relies on – some of the most important flavours also come from bulbs, roots and tubers including ginger, onions, shallots, turmeric and tamarind (above left). And completing the fragrant contributors to this cuisine – herbs, chillies and exotic fruit and vegetables such as mango and rose (above right).

Because it is so flavourful, and contains a large number of ingredients, Indian cooking is often passed over as being too complicated. This need not be the case with a Thermomix® to help you! It's not only the grinding of spices you'll find it invaluable for, but it speeds any Indian recipe up by chopping all those ingredients in a matter of seconds. There's less washing up, too, when you use the self-wash function*. You're also saving yourself the time of standing over a hob stirring.

* Place 1000 g warm water in mixing bowl and a drop of washing up liquid, then allow it to wash **3 min/speed 5**. Depending on how dirty the bowl is, you can set it for longer, and/or have it on 50°C.

Equipment

Owning a Thermomix® means you won't need a lot of traditional Indian utensils, such as iron balti pans, pestle and mortars or woks. However, there are a few items you may still find useful, such as kulfi moulds for the dessert on page 162. There are many varieties available online.

We also use a muslin cloth for various recipes, including paneer (page 28).

Cake tins or plates can be raised using a steaming rack (available online or in Asian stores) or chopsticks (broken in half if too long), or large cookie cutters.

How to use this book

In the first chapter you'll find some basic staples for Indian cooking, such as ghee, paneer and coconut milk. Although you can buy most of these ingredients, you'll probably find it far more satisfying (and less expensive!) to create your entire dish from scratch.

As far as meal planning goes, you may wish to make just one curry and a rice dish for a midweek meal for two. Alternatively, if you have friends coming round for a curry night, why not create your own Indian feast? You could prepare some starters, a combination of meat and vegetarian main and side dishes, and perhaps some rice and naan on the side, all washed down with an Indian lassi before finishing with a sweet treat. We've provided you with recipes for condiments as well, including the classic mango chutney, and recipes like these can be made in advance.

SPICE LEVELS

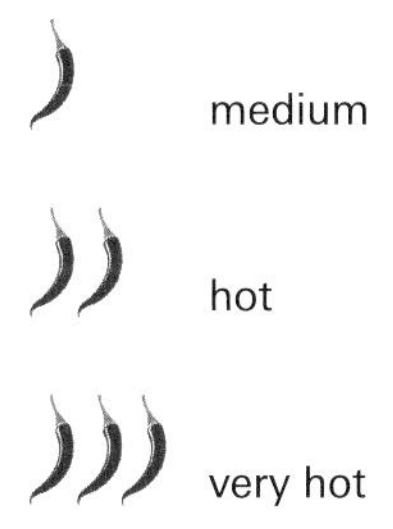

medium

hot

very hot

We have allocated a spice rating to those recipes which pack a bit more heat. We hope this will provide you with a guide as to how hot or spicy each dish is. No rating means the dish is mild or has no heat, such as a korma. One chilli implies there is a low level of heat, two chillies a hot dish and three chillies mark the spiciest dishes.

All our recipes are written and tested using fan assisted ovens.

Gas	Electric (°C)	Fan (°C)
1	140	120
2	150	130
3	170	150
4	180	160
5	190	170
6	200	180
7	220	200
8	230	210
9	240	220

Ingredients and icons

- Always use **good quality ingredients,** preferably fresh unless otherwise mentioned in the recipe.

- **Frozen** ingredients (e. g. prawns, peas) can be an excellent shortcut in certain recipes.

- Where 'cut in pieces' is instructed, and to achieve **uniform results,** cut ingredients in evenly-sized pieces, no larger than 5 cm x 5 cm when placing them in mixing bowl.

- Always refer to the **tips and variations** for help with hard-to-find ingredients.

- **Homemade vs. shop-bought ingredients:** some of the ingredients used in the recipes can be very simply made in the Thermomix®, such as ghee, paneer, coconut milk and spice mixes. We have indicated these easy-to-make ingredients with this icon: 👆. You'll find recipes for them throughout this book.

- **For successful recipes, and for your safety,** adhere to the quantities specified in the recipes. Never exceed the maximum capacity of the mixing bowl, 2.2 l and of the Varoma, 3.3 l.

- The **weight** of ingredients in recipes refers to ready-to-use ingredients, where necessary. For instance, clean leeks or peel potatoes and onions before weighing.

- **Volume measurements:** For small quantities of strong ingredients such as salt or sesame oil, we measure in tsp or Tbsp. One standard Tbsp is 15 ml (= 15 g water), and 1 tsp is 5 ml (= 5 g water). If using measuring spoons, make sure contents are level with edge of spoon.

- **Unless otherwise mentioned:**
  - **Eggs** are European medium size (53 – 63 g, USA and Canada: large) and at room temperature.
  - **Butter** is unsalted and chilled.
  - **Milk** is full-fat or semi-skimmed, not skimmed.
  - **Cream** is full-fat (min. 30% fat), e. g. whipping or double.
  - **Flour** or plain flour is white wheat flour (approx. 10-11% protein). For bread dough, use bread flour or strong flour.
  - **Sugar** is white granulated sugar, which can often be replaced with raw unrefined sugar.
  - **Oil** is sunflower oil. Vegetable oil can be used instead.
  - **Dry yeast** is instant yeast which can be mixed into the recipe without rehydration.
  - **'Adjust seasoning to taste'** means add salt, pepper or other seasonings to your preference.

ICONS USED IN THE RECIPES

Active time
This is the hands-on time you have to invest to prepare the recipe.

Total time
This shows the total time needed to prepare the dish until the moment it can be served. Total time also includes baking times, cooling times etc.

Difficulty
You should be able to master all the recipes without any problems. Some of them are more challenging than others, and may require more of your time if you are new to cooking.

Servings
This shows how many portions or pieces the recipe makes.

Nutritional value
The nutritional values are based on averages. The real nutritional values of your dish may differ based on the ingredients you choose.

BASICS

GHEE

Ghee is clarified butter and you can easily make your own. Ghee has a very high smoke point, so is excellent for frying with. It also keeps for longer than butter. Although high in saturated fats, it is considered to possess a host of health benefits.

INGREDIENTS

250 g unsalted butter, diced

USEFUL ITEMS

fine sieve
sterilised jar or container

PREPARATION

1. Place butter in mixing bowl and cook **10 min/Varoma/speed** ↺.
   Leave to cool for 5 minutes.
2. Pour through a fine sieve into a warm, sterilised jar or container discarding any white solids.
3. Seal and label then cool to room temperature before storing in fridge. Use as required in Indian dishes.

5 min  20 min  easy 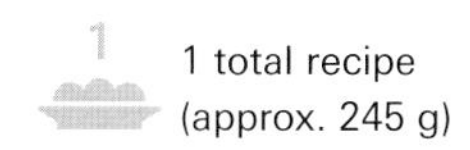 1 total recipe (approx. 245 g)

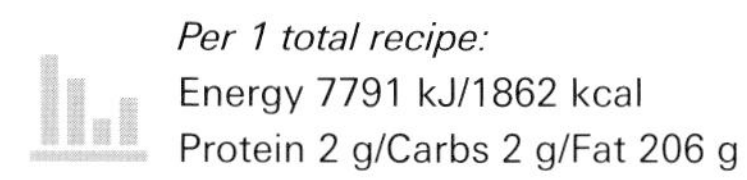

Per 1 total recipe:
Energy 7791 kJ/1862 kcal
Protein 2 g/Carbs 2 g/Fat 206 g

GARAM MASALA

This useful, aromatic blend of ground spices varies regionally, but something common to all recipes is that the ingredients are toasted before being ground. The toasting process heightens the flavours by releasing fragrant oils. This frequently used base brings warmth and flavour to many dishes, including rogan josh. Freshly ground in your Thermomix®, it will transform any dish.

INGREDIENTS

½ cinnamon stick
2 Tbsp coriander seeds
2 Tbsp cumin seeds
2 tsp black peppercorns
1 tsp cardamom seeds or ground cardamom
1 tsp dried fennel seeds
1 tsp whole cloves
2-4 dried bay leaves, or dried curry leaves, to taste

USEFUL ITEMS

airtight jar or container

PREPARATION

1. Place all ingredients in mixing bowl and toast **3 min/120°C/speed 1**.
2. Grind **1 min 30 sec/speed 10**. Transfer to an airtight jar or container, seal and label then store until needed.

5 min  10 min  easy  1 total recipe (approx. 35 g)

Per 1 total recipe:
Energy 1519 kJ/363 kcal
Protein 13 g/Carbs 46 g/Fat 14 g

MADRAS CURRY POWDER

This earthy, fragrant blend of spices forms a base for Madras-style curries. It can also be used to add extra flavour and colour to soups or broths. Like many Indian spice mixtures, there are many variations but this recipe is a well-balanced blend of the key spices.

INGREDIENTS

5 dried red chillies
2½ Tbsp coriander seeds
1 Tbsp cumin seeds
1 Tbsp black peppercorns
1 Tbsp fine sea salt
2 tsp ground turmeric
2 tsp yellow mustard seeds
2 tsp garlic powder
1 tsp ground ginger
1 tsp whole allspice berries
1 pinch saffron threads (optional)

USEFUL ITEMS

airtight jar or container

PREPARATION

1. Place all ingredients in mixing bowl and grind **10 sec/speed 10**. Transfer to an airtight jar or container, seal and label then store until needed.

VARIATION

- Try adding fennel seeds, fenugreek seeds or dried curry leaves as desired.

5 min

5 min

easy

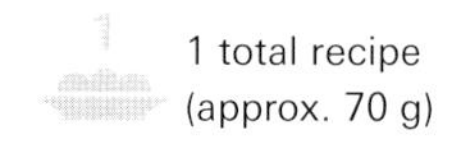

1 total recipe (approx. 70 g)

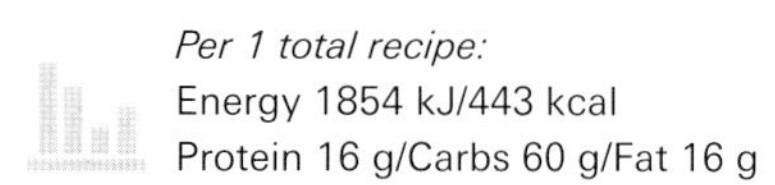

Per 1 total recipe:
Energy 1854 kJ/443 kcal
Protein 16 g/Carbs 60 g/Fat 16 g

TIKKA PASTE

A very popular recipe, this paste can be used to make a quick curry with the meat of your choice (see page 56). It is a must-have ingredient to keep in your kitchen and this recipe makes plenty – will store for up to a month in the fridge, or frozen in small batches for up to three months.

INGREDIENTS

40 g coriander seeds
40 g cumin seeds
5-6 dried Kashmiri chillies, to taste
1 Tbsp black peppercorns
50 g fresh coriander, leaves and stalks
100 g garlic cloves
100 g fresh root ginger, peeled, cut in round slices (2 mm)
220 g vegetable oil, plus extra for preserving
100 g water
100 g lemon juice
30 g fine sea salt
50 g dried onions
140 g tomato purée
1 tsp ground turmeric
1 tsp Kashmiri chilli powder
1 tsp garam masala

USEFUL ITEMS

sterilised jam jars

PREPARATION

1. Place coriander seeds, cumin seeds, chillies and peppercorns in mixing bowl then toast **5 min/Varoma/speed 1**. Grind **1 min/speed 8**.
2. Add fresh coriander, garlic, ginger and oil then blend **1 min/speed 10**. Scrape down sides and lid of mixing bowl with spatula.
3. Add water, lemon juice, salt, dried onions, tomato purée, turmeric, chilli powder and garam masala then cook **45 min/80°C/speed 2**.
4. Transfer to warm sterilised jars, adding a little oil if necessary to cover the paste (see tip). Seal and label then, when cool, store in fridge until needed.

TIP

- Top up with a little more oil after each use so the paste stays submerged; this helps to preserve it.

 15 min

 1 hour

 easy

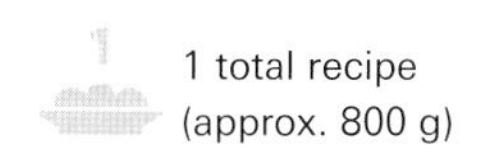 1 total recipe (approx. 800 g)

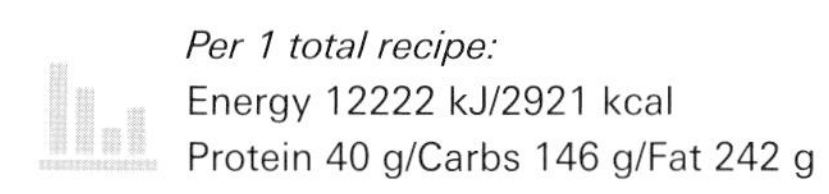
Per 1 total recipe:
Energy 12222 kJ/2921 kcal
Protein 40 g/Carbs 146 g/Fat 242 g

TAMARIND PASTE

Tamarind is a sticky, sour fruit that grows in pods in tropical climates. It is a staple of Indian households where it is frequently used as a condiment (when thinned and flavoured), as a snack, and as an accompaniment to starters and main dishes. Also, widely used in other cuisines including Thai and Mexican, tamarind paste can be made for a fraction of the cost of buying it, and it is much more satisfying knowing you have made it yourself in your Thermomix®.

INGREDIENTS

200 g dried tamarind, in pieces
600 g water, boiling

USEFUL ITEMS

sterilised jam jars

PREPARATION

1. Place tamarind and boiling water in mixing bowl then cook **7 min/80°C/speed 1**.
2. Mix **30 sec/speed 6**, then pour into simmering basket set over a bowl.
3. Press mixture against simmering basket with a spatula to extract paste and collect in bowl below. Discard fibre and seeds in simmering basket. Transfer paste to warm, sterilised jars then seal, label and allow to cool. Store in fridge and use as required in Indian recipes.

TIPS

- The paste can be kept in the fridge for up to a month or stored in the freezer for up to 3 months.
- A block of 'wet' tamarind can be used instead of a dried block, following exactly the same method.

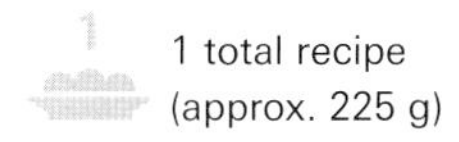
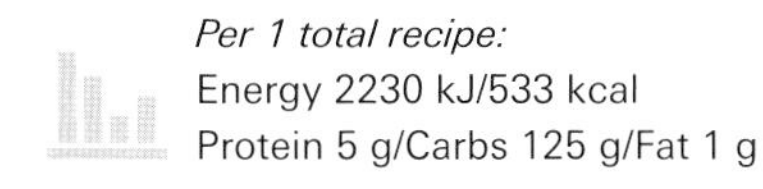

5 min | 15 min | easy | 1 total recipe (approx. 225 g)

Per 1 total recipe:
Energy 2230 kJ/533 kcal
Protein 5 g/Carbs 125 g/Fat 1 g

PANEER

This non-melting, white curd cheese is very commonly used in Indian dishes as a vegetarian option. It is incredibly versatile and is easily made in the Thermomix® with just two ingredients.

INGREDIENTS

2000 g whole milk
3 Tbsp lemon juice or vinegar (white wine vinegar or cider vinegar)

USEFUL ITEMS

large bowl
fine sieve or nut milk bag
muslin cloth
heavy weight

PREPARATION

1. Place milk in mixing bowl and heat **20 min/90°C/speed 2**.
2. Add lemon juice and mix **1 min/speed 2,** during which time the milk will separate into curds and whey.
3. Place a muslin cloth inside a fine sieve, or use a nut milk bag, over a large bowl. Pour mixture into muslin or bag. Allow to drain for 1-2 hours, collecting curds in muslin or bag and whey in bowl below.
4. After this time, squeeze muslin or nut milk bag so remaining whey drips into bowl.
5. Place muslin or bag in simmering basket inside a bowl, keeping hold of the ends. Twist ends together tightly then flatten down over curd ball. Place a heavy weight on top allowing whey to continue to drip from curd.
6. After 3-4 hours, curds will have formed a solid disc of paneer. Store in fridge for up to 3 days, using in pieces in Indian main courses, snacks and desserts.

TIP

- The whey can be used to make chapati or paratha dough. It can also be used to cook rice or dal.

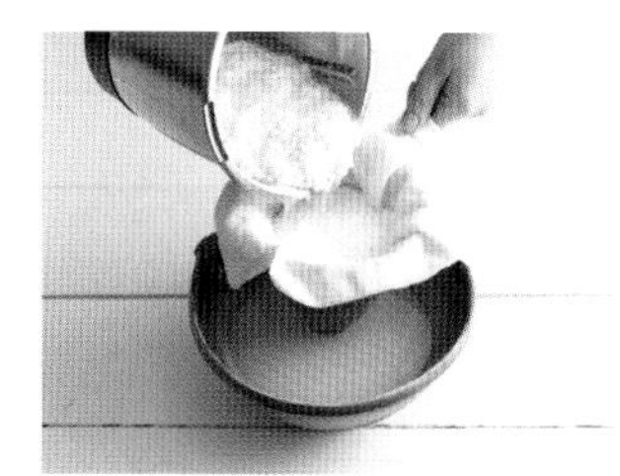
Step 3

Step 4

Step 5

 15 min

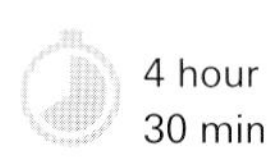 4 hour 30 min

 easy

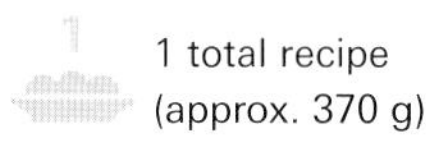 1 total recipe (approx. 370 g)

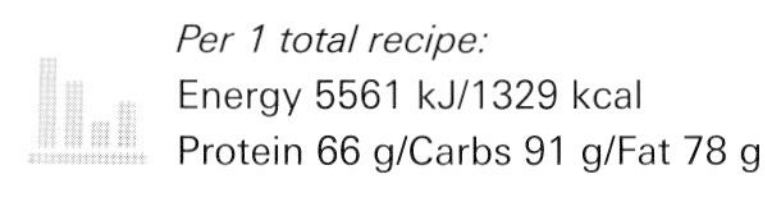
Per 1 total recipe:
Energy 5561 kJ/1329 kcal
Protein 66 g/Carbs 91 g/Fat 78 g

COCONUT MILK

Coconut milk is widely used in Indian cuisine, especially in areas such as Goa and Gujarat, and can be made very easily and efficiently in your Thermomix®. It is great for vegans and those intolerant to lactose. Although high in saturated fats, it is believed to be high in vitamins and fibre and helps boost the immune system.

INGREDIENTS
150 g coconut flesh, fresh, peeled, cut in pieces (3 cm)
450 g water

USEFUL ITEMS
glass bottle
fine sieve or nut milk bag
muslin cloth
large bowl

PREPARATION
1. Place coconut flesh in mixing bowl and grate **5 sec/speed 8.** Scrape down sides of mixing bowl with spatula.
2. Add water and cook **5 min/100°C/speed 4**, then blend **30 sec/speed 8**.
3. Place a muslin cloth inside a fine sieve, or use a nut milk bag, over a large bowl. Pour coconut water into muslin or bag, collecting milk in bowl below. Leave to cool then squeeze and wring out muslin or bag until all coconut milk is extracted, reserving pulp (see tip). Transfer milk to a glass bottle and store in fridge. Use as desired.

TIPS
- Homemade coconut milk will last for 3-4 days in the fridge. As there are no preservatives the cream may separate out. Shake bottle before using.
- The leftover coconut pulp can be dried and used to make coconut flour.

VARIATIONS
- To make double the quantity, use 300 g fresh coconut flesh and 900 g water. In step 2 cook 7 **min/100°C/speed 4**.
- Desiccated coconut can be used instead of fresh coconut. For 150 g desiccated coconut use 900 g water.

10 min

20 min

easy
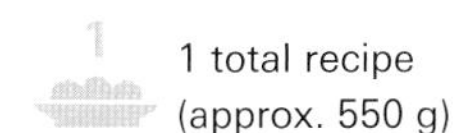
1 total recipe (approx. 550 g)
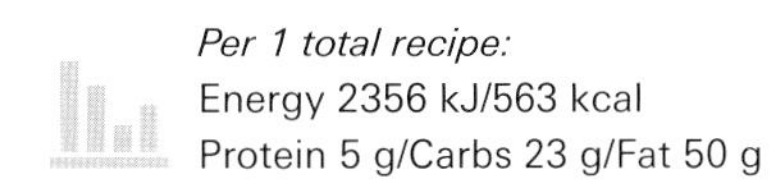
Per 1 total recipe:
Energy 2356 kJ/563 kcal
Protein 5 g/Carbs 23 g/Fat 50 g

STARTERS AND LIGHT MEALS

CURRIED RHUBARB AND LENTIL SOUP

This recipe sits somewhere between a dal and a soup, and we think it would make an excellent lunch option if you fancy something spiced. Although usually found in sweet dishes, rhubarb is in fact a vegetable, and adds a sharp tone set against the earthy lentils and spices.

INGREDIENTS

- 1 tsp coriander seeds
- 1 tsp cumin seeds
- 30 g vegetable oil
- 150 g onions, quartered
- 150 g celery stalks, cut in pieces
- 3 garlic cloves
- 1½ tsp garam masala 👆
- 1 tsp paprika
- 1 tsp ground ginger
- ¼ tsp ground turmeric
- 350 g rhubarb, cut in pieces (1 cm)
- 150 g chana dal (yellow dried split peas)
- 700 g water
- 1 vegetable stock cube (for 0.5 l)
- 30 g brown sugar
- ½ tsp fine sea salt, or to taste
- ¼ tsp ground black pepper, or to taste
- 40 g plain yoghurt, for serving
- 3 sprigs fresh coriander, leaves only, chopped, for serving

PREPARATION

1. Place coriander and cumin seeds in mixing bowl then toast **3 min/Varoma/speed 2**. Grind **2 min/speed 10**. Transfer to a small bowl and set aside.
2. Place oil, onions, celery and garlic in mixing bowl then chop **5 sec/speed 5**. Scrape down sides of mixing bowl with spatula then sauté **5 min/100°C/speed 1**.
3. Add garam masala, paprika, ginger, turmeric and reserved ground spices then sauté **2 min/100°C/speed 1**.
4. Add rhubarb, chana dal, water and stock cube then cook **30 min/100°C/↺/speed 0.5**.
5. Add sugar, salt and pepper then, replace measuring cup with simmering basket, and cook again **30 min/100°C/↺/speed 0.5**.
6. Transfer to serving bowls, garnish with yoghurt and chopped, fresh coriander leaves then serve.

10 min

1 hour 20 min

easy

4 portions

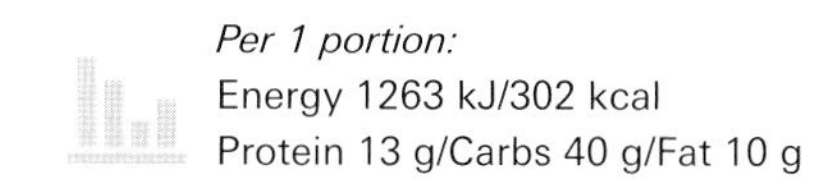

Per 1 portion:
Energy 1263 kJ/302 kcal
Protein 13 g/Carbs 40 g/Fat 10 g

SAMBHAR

This pulse-based vegetable soup originates from south India and is often served with rice or dosas, but it makes an excellent starter or accompaniment to an Indian spread of curries and rice. You can substitute the vegetables to your taste.

INGREDIENTS

50 g onions, quartered
50 g tomatoes, halved

Masala

25 g vegetable oil
1 tsp chana dal or toor dal (yellow dried split peas)
1 tsp fenugreek seeds
1 tsp black mustard seeds
1 tsp asafoetida
2-4 dried Kashmiri chillies, to taste

Soup

5 cm dried tamarind, soaked in hot water for 15 minutes
1200 g water
150 g chana dal or toor dal (yellow dried split peas)
100 g aubergines, cut in pieces (2 cm)
100 g butternut squash, peeled, cut in pieces (2 cm)
100 g fine green beans, cut in pieces (2 cm)
1½ tsp ground turmeric
1½ tsp sugar
1½ tsp fine sea salt

USEFUL ITEMS

fine sieve

PREPARATION

1. Place onions and tomatoes in mixing bowl then chop **3 sec/speed 5**. Transfer to a bowl and set aside.

Masala

2. Place oil in mixing bowl and heat **2 min/85°C/speed 0.5**.
3. Add chana dal, fenugreek seeds, mustard seeds, asafoetida and chillies then fry **3 min/85°C/speed 0.5**. Blend to a paste **1 min/speed 10**. Transfer to a bowl and set aside.

Soup

4. Strain soaked tamarind through a fine sieve collecting tamarind water below. Discard pulp and set tamarind water aside.
5. Place water in mixing bowl and bring to the boil **8 min/100°C/speed 1**.
6. Add chana dal, aubergines, butternut squash, green beans and reserved chopped onions and tomatoes. Replace measuring cup with simmering basket, then simmer **20 min/95°C/↺/speed 0.5**.
7. Add turmeric, sugar, salt and 2 Tbsp reserved tamarind water. Replace measuring cup with simmering basket and simmer **15 min/95°C/↺/speed 0.5**.
8. Add reserved masala paste and stir **1 min/90°C/↺/speed 1**. Serve hot with Indian bread of choice.

VARIATION

- Sambhar can be served with a tarka, which is made by adding spices to very hot oil. The spice seeds pop and sizzle bringing out their intense flavour and aroma. For this recipe, a tarka made from fried onions, mustard seeds and fenugreek seeds added to hot oil and stirred in just before serving would work well.

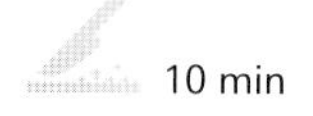
10 min

1 hour 5 min

easy

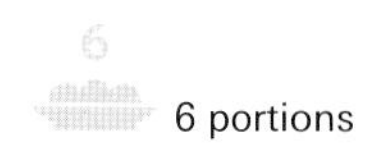
6 portions

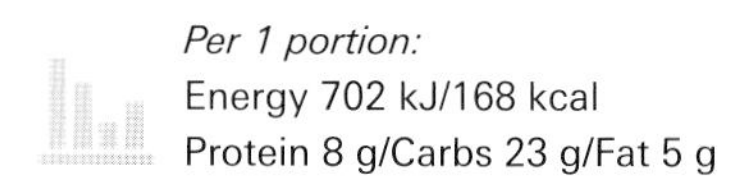
Per 1 portion:
Energy 702 kJ/168 kcal
Protein 8 g/Carbs 23 g/Fat 5 g

BAINGAN BHURTA (AUBERGINE BHURTA)

This is a popular vegetarian option from Gujarat where traditionally the Hindus were strict vegetarians. Leaving the aubergine skins on gives the dish a nice texture and colour, but you can peel them if you prefer a smoother result. It makes a delicious light lunch with chapatis or naan bread, although can also be eaten as part of a main meal.

INGREDIENTS

500 g water
500 g aubergines, cut in pieces (3 cm)
1 garlic clove
250 g onions, quartered
30 g vegetable oil
1 tsp ground cumin
1 tsp fine sea salt
½ tsp ground black pepper

PREPARATION

1. Place water in mixing bowl. Place Varoma dish into position and weigh in aubergines. Cover and steam **15 min/Varoma/speed 1**. Set Varoma aside and discard steaming water.
2. Place garlic in mixing bowl and chop **5 sec/speed 8**.
3. Add onions and chop **3 sec/speed 5**. Scrape down sides of mixing bowl with spatula.
4. Add oil and cumin then, without measuring cup, sauté **3 min/120°C/speed 1**.
5. Add reserved steamed aubergine, salt and pepper then, with measuring cup in place, chop **6 sec/speed 5**. Scrape down sides of mixing bowl with spatula then cook **2 min/100°C/speed 3**. Serve warm with your favourite Indian bread.

10 min

30 min

easy

6 portions

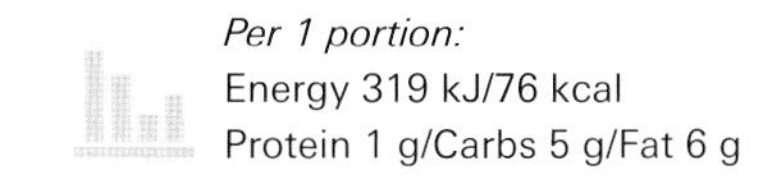

Per 1 portion:
Energy 319 kJ/76 kcal
Protein 1 g/Carbs 5 g/Fat 6 g

ONION BHAJI

Traditionally served as a snack in India ('bhajia'), often with a cup of chai, this spiced onion fritter is a popular starter dish on Indian menus in the UK and Ireland. This recipe will ensure you have crispy, flavourful results every time.

INGREDIENTS

85 g gram flour
50 g plain yoghurt
1 large egg
1 Tbsp garam masala
1 Tbsp dried fenugreek leaves
1 Tbsp lemon juice
1 tsp ground cumin
1 tsp fine sea salt
1 tsp Kashmiri chilli powder
35 g water
300 g onions, large, thinly sliced (2 mm)
vegetable oil, for deep frying

USEFUL ITEMS

deep saucepan or deep fat fryer
slotted spoon
paper towel

PREPARATION

1. Place flour, yoghurt, egg, garam masala, dried fenugreek leaves, lemon juice, cumin, salt and chilli powder in mixing bowl then mix **10 sec/speed 4**. Scrape down sides of mixing bowl with spatula.
2. Add water and mix **10 sec/speed 4**.
3. Add sliced onions and mix **10 sec/⟲/speed 2**. Scrape down sides of mixing bowl and stir with spatula. Allow mixture to stand for 10 minutes. Meanwhile, preheat oil in a deep fat fryer or deep, heavy based saucepan to 190°C.
4. Stir onion mixture well, then using two heat-proof, long-handled spoons, gently place 1 tablespoon-sized clumps of battered onions into hot oil. Fry in batches for 4-6 minutes (190°C), turning to ensure even cooking. Remove from oil with a slotted spoon and drain on paper towel. Serve hot with salad garnish, raita, chutneys or lemon wedges.

TIP

- Bhajis can be allowed to cool, then frozen. When you are ready to serve, reheat thawed bhajis in deep, hot oil for about 2 minutes but don't let them get too brown. Serve hot.

VARIATION

- Also works well with red onions.

40 min

45 min

medium

18 pieces
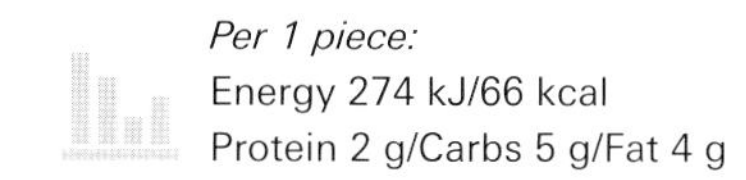
Per 1 piece:
Energy 274 kJ/66 kcal
Protein 2 g/Carbs 5 g/Fat 4 g

VEGETABLE SAMOSA FILLING

Samosas are said to originate from Moghul times, and are a very popular street food in India. Use this filling for the samosa pastry recipe on page 44. Serve hot with fresh Indian chutney, such as coriander (page 128).

INGREDIENTS

100 g onions, quartered
2 garlic cloves
1 tsp black mustard seeds
1 tsp fine sea salt
1 tsp ground cumin
1 tsp ground coriander
1 tsp amchoor (mango powder) or 1 Tbsp lemon juice
¼ tsp ground turmeric
1 Tbsp groundnut oil
200 g water
150 g potatoes, peeled, diced (1 cm)
80 g cauliflower, cut in pieces (1 cm) (optional)
80 g red split lentils, rinsed
70 g frozen green peas

PREPARATION

1. Place onions and garlic in mixing bowl then chop **3 sec/speed 7.** Scrape down sides of mixing bowl with spatula.
2. Add mustard seeds, salt, cumin, coriander, amchoor, turmeric and oil then sauté **5 min/100°C/speed 0.5**.
3. Add water, potatoes, cauliflower (if using) and lentils then cook **5 min/100°C/↺/speed 0.5**. Scrape down sides of mixing bowl with spatula then cook again **10 min/100°C/↺/speed 0.5**.
4. Add frozen peas and stir in with spatula. Transfer to a bowl and set aside to cool.
5. Use cooled filling with samosa pastry (see recipe page 44) for vegetable samosas.

5 min

30 min

easy

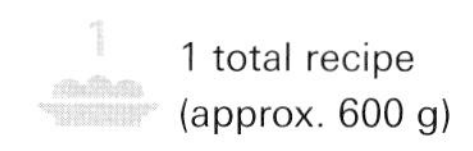
1 total recipe (approx. 600 g)

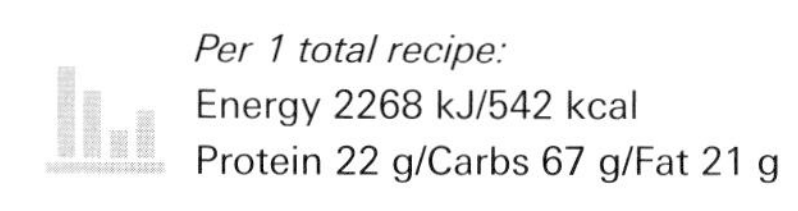
Per 1 total recipe:
Energy 2268 kJ/542 kcal
Protein 22 g/Carbs 67 g/Fat 21 g

TRADITIONAL SAMOSA

Pastry is a complete breeze with Thermomix®, and samosa pastry is no different! These triangular, savoury crispy pastries come in many varieties, shapes and sizes. They can be prepared with many different fillings, too, including minced meat, vegetables (see page 42) or even chocolate for a dessert version!

INGREDIENTS

170 g water
270 g plain flour
80 g groundnut oil or rapeseed oil
1 pinch fine sea salt
vegetable oil, for deep frying

USEFUL ITEMS

jug
cling film
rolling pin
deep saucepan or deep fat fryer
baking tray
slotted spoon
paper towel

PREPARATION

1. Place a jug on mixing bowl lid and weigh in 100 g water. Set jug aside.
2. Place 230 g flour, oil and salt in mixing bowl then mix **15 sec/speed 3**.
3. Without measuring cup, and without setting a time, mix **speed 2** while slowly adding water from jug through hole in mixing bowl lid, stopping when dough comes together. With measuring cup in place, knead **3 min/** then tip out onto work surface, form into a ball, wrap in cling film and chill in fridge for 30 minutes.
4. Meanwhile, place a small bowl on mixing bowl lid and weigh in remaining 40 g flour and 70 g water. Remove from lid and mix together until a paste; this will be used as 'glue'.
5. After 30 minutes when dough has rested, tip out onto a work surface and divide into 12 equal-sized pieces. Shape into balls then roll each into a circle as thin as possible (approx. 1 mm). Cut each circle in half.
6. Preheat oil in a deep fat fryer or deep, heavy based saucepan to 190°C.
7. Meanwhile, take a semi-circle of pastry and, using a finger, spread 'glue' around the edges. With the straight edge towards you, place 1 Tbsp samosa filling (see page 42 for recipe) in middle of semi-circle and fold left corner up towards the middle (covering samosa filling). Fold right corner over to form a cone shape and ensure samosa filling is evenly spread within pocket before sealing curved edge of samosa. Set aside on a baking tray. Repeat with remaining pastry and filling.
8. Cook samosas, in batches, in preheated oil for 3-4 minutes (190°C) until golden, turning to ensure even cooking. Remove with a slotted spoon and drain on paper towel. Serve warm as a starter.

55 min

1 hour 30 min

advanced

24 pieces

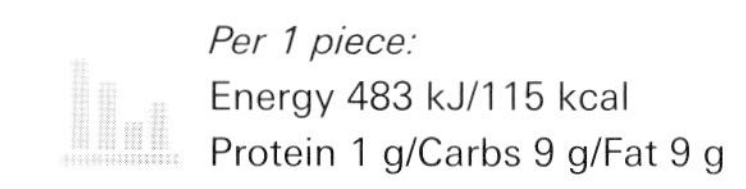

Per 1 piece:
Energy 483 kJ/115 kcal
Protein 1 g/Carbs 9 g/Fat 9 g

Step 7

PURI

This simple, unleavened, deep-fried bread is often eaten for breakfast, lunch or as a light snack. It would also work well served as a starter or canapé topped with prawn bhuna (page 98).

INGREDIENTS

225 g chapati flour or wholemeal flour, plus extra, for dusting
25 g ghee
¼ tsp fine sea salt
150 g water, warm
vegetable oil, for deep frying

USEFUL ITEMS

jug
rolling pin
slotted spoon
paper towel
deep saucepan or deep fat fryer

PREPARATION

1. Place flour, ghee and salt in mixing bowl.
2. Place a jug on mixing bowl lid and weigh in water. Remove jug, then, without measuring cup, and without setting a time, mix **speed 2** while slowly adding water through hole in mixing bowl lid, stopping when dough comes together. Insert measuring cup then knead **3 min/**. Meanwhile, preheat oil in a deep fat fryer or deep, heavy based saucepan to 190°C.
3. Tip dough out onto a floured work surface. Divide into 16 equal-sized pieces. Shape into balls then roll out to 16 discs (Ø 10 cm).
4. Fry each puri for 30 seconds (190°C) – they will sink and then rise back up to indicate they are cooked. Remove with a slotted spoon then drain on paper towel while cooking remaining puris.
5. Serve as an accompaniment to Indian dishes.

TIP

- Wrap cooked puris in foil and keep warm in an oven set to 100°C until ready to serve.

30 min

35 min

easy

16 pieces
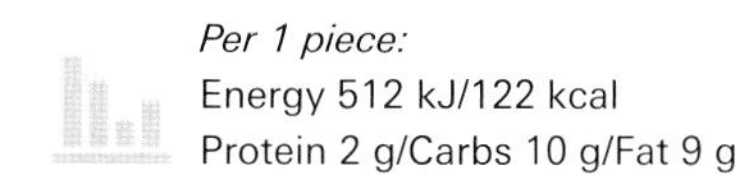
Per 1 piece:
Energy 512 kJ/122 kcal
Protein 2 g/Carbs 10 g/Fat 9 g

SHEEK KEBAB

Kebabs come in many shapes, from barbecued in a tandoor to deep-fried or in a curry sauce. The mixture can be whizzed up in seconds in the Thermomix®, and this simple recipe would make a terrific lunch option served with chutney and raita.

INGREDIENTS

20 g fresh coriander leaves
5 g fresh mint leaves
120 g onions, quartered
2-3 garlic cloves, to taste
1-2 fresh green chillies, halved, deseeded, to taste
500 g lamb mince, broken in pieces
20 g lemon juice
1½ tsp ground turmeric
1½ tsp ground coriander
1½ tsp ground cumin
1 tsp garam masala
1 tsp paprika
1 tsp fine sea salt
1 Tbsp vegetable oil, for greasing

USEFUL ITEMS

wooden skewers
cling film
pastry brush
grill pan with wire rack

PREPARATION

1. Soak 12 wooden skewers in water for at least 30 minutes. Meanwhile, place coriander and mint leaves in mixing bowl then chop **3 sec/speed 8**. Scrape down sides of mixing bowl with spatula.
2. Add onions, garlic and chillies then chop **3 sec/speed 7**. Scrape down sides of mixing bowl with spatula.
3. Add lamb mince, lemon juice, turmeric, coriander, cumin, garam masala, paprika and salt then mix **5 sec/speed 3**. Scrape down sides of mixing bowl with spatula then mix again **5 sec/speed 3**.
4. With wet hands, divide mixture into 12 equal-sized pieces then, form kebabs (about 10 cm long) on pre-soaked skewers. Arrange on a plate, cover with cling film and refrigerate for 15 minutes. Meanwhile, preheat grill to 230°C.
5. Brush kebabs with oil then place on a wire rack over a grill pan. Cook for 15-20 minutes (230°C) directly under hot grill, turning occasionally until cooked through. Serve hot with baingan raita (page 130) or coriander chutney (page 128).

TIP

- Can also be cooked on a barbecue for 15-20 minutes, turning occasionally.

20 min

1 hour 10 min

easy

12 pieces

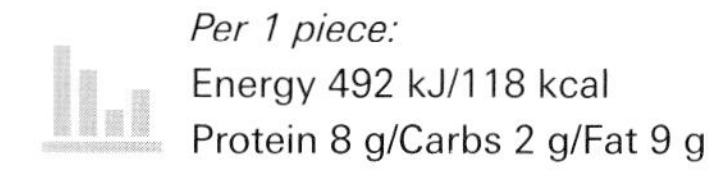
Per 1 piece:
Energy 492 kJ/118 kcal
Protein 8 g/Carbs 2 g/Fat 9 g

ALOO BEETROOT TIKKI

The beetroot provides a refreshing, healthier twist on these traditional little potato-based patties. They make a delicious light meal with salad and chutney, or as part of a larger Indian banquet.

INGREDIENTS

1000 g water
350 g potatoes, peeled, cut in pieces (2 cm)
70 g onions, quartered
15 g vegetable oil, plus extra for frying
1 fresh green chilli, halved, deseeded
100 g cooked beetroot, quartered
1 tsp Kashmiri chilli powder
1 tsp garam masala
1 tsp fine sea salt
1 Tbsp plain flour, for dusting

USEFUL ITEMS

paper towel
frying pan

PREPARATION

1. Place water in mixing bowl. Insert simmering basket and weigh in potatoes then steam **15 min/Varoma/speed 2.5**. Remove simmering basket with aid of spatula and discard water from mixing bowl.
2. Place onions, oil and fresh chilli in mixing bowl then chop **5 sec/speed 5**. Scrape down sides of mixing bowl with spatula then sauté **5 min/Varoma/speed** .
3. Add beetroot, chilli powder, garam masala, salt and reserved steamed potatoes then mash **2 sec/speed 5**. Transfer to a bowl and leave to cool completely in fridge.
4. Once mixture is cool, with wet hands, form 10 small, round patties (Ø 5 cm). Dust lightly with flour then place on a floured plate.
5. Heat a little oil in a frying pan over a medium heat. Fry patties in batches for 3-5 minutes on each side until browned. Drain on paper towel. Serve warm with pickles, chutneys or yoghurt.

TIP

- For a smoother mixture, increase mashing time in step 3 to **3 sec/speed 5**.

20 min

1 hour

easy

10 pieces

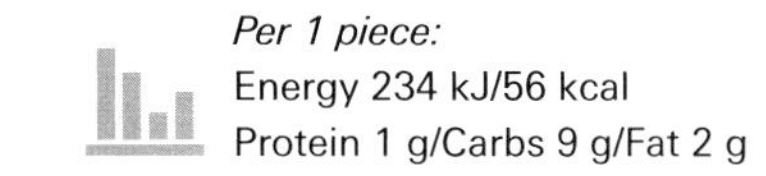
Per 1 piece:
Energy 234 kJ/56 kcal
Protein 1 g/Carbs 9 g/Fat 2 g

DHOKLA

This light, fluffy, savoury steamed cake is incredibly versatile and can be served as a snack, starter or side dish. Originating in Gujarat, it is traditionally made with rice and lentils but this quick version uses semolina and is known in the west as 'instant' dhokla.

INGREDIENTS

½ tsp vegetable oil, for greasing
2 fresh green chillies, halved
2 garlic cloves
15 g fresh coriander leaves
150 g semolina
180 g plain yoghurt
1120 g water
1 tsp fine sea salt
1 tsp bicarbonate of soda

USEFUL ITEMS

round cake tin (Ø 20 cm)
baking paper
wooden skewers

PREPARATION

1. Grease and line base of a round cake tin (Ø 20 cm) with baking paper.
2. Place chillies, garlic and coriander in mixing bowl then mince **3 sec/speed 9**. Scrape down sides and lid of mixing bowl with spatula.
3. Add semolina, yoghurt, 120 g water, salt and bicarbonate of soda then mix **15 sec/speed 4**. Transfer to prepared cake tin.
4. Place remaining 1000 g water in mixing bowl and place Varoma dish into position. Arrange 2 wooden skewers, cut to fit (approx. 19 cm), in Varoma dish. Rest cake tin on top of skewers ensuring it is level then cover and steam **20 min/Varoma/speed 1**. Set Varoma aside and remove Varoma lid then allow to stand for 3 minutes before serving.

TIPS

- Using wooden skewers in the base of the Varoma dish creates a trivet for the cake tin to stand on. This enables the steam to circulate evenly around the tin without any obstructions.
- Serve with pickles or chutneys and salad, or as an accompaniment to curries.
- Can be served warm or at room temperature.

Step 4

 5 min  30 min  easy  10 portions 

Per 1 portion:
Energy 282 kJ/68 kcal
Protein 3 g/Carbs 12 g/Fat 1 g

MAINS – MEAT

CHICKEN TIKKA

These 'little pieces' (the literal translation of 'tikka') of chicken were not commonly found here until the 1970s when tandoori cooking spread rapidly to most curry houses. Traditionally baked on a skewer in a clay oven, these tasty little chicken chunks can be served hot or cold either as they are or stirred into a masala sauce to make chicken tikka masala (page 58) – one of the UK and Ireland's most popular dishes!

INGREDIENTS

500 g chicken breasts, skinless, sliced (2 cm)
100 g plain yoghurt
150 g Tikka paste
vegetable oil, for greasing

USEFUL ITEMS

cling film
metal skewers
baking tray
aluminium foil

PREPARATION

1. Place a bowl on mixing bowl lid and weigh in chicken pieces, yoghurt and Tikka paste. Remove bowl from lid and stir well so that chicken is coated. Cover and refrigerate for at least 3 hours or overnight.
2. Preheat grill to 230°C. Line a baking tray with foil and grease with vegetable oil. Thread marinated chicken pieces onto metal skewers and grill for 10-12 minutes (230°C), turning occasionally until browned and cooked through. Serve with rice or Indian bread, kachumber (page 126) and chutneys, or see chicken tikka masala, page 58.

TIP

- The chicken pieces can also be grilled without skewers. Instead, place directly on baking tray lined with foil, turning pieces of chicken with tongs during grilling so evenly browned and cooked.

VARIATION

- Diced paneer, vegetables, prawns or lamb could be used in place of chicken. Grilling time will vary.

30 min

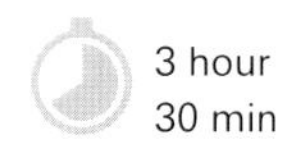
3 hour
30 min

easy

4 portions

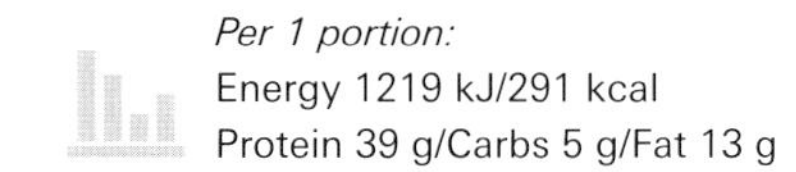
Per 1 portion:
Energy 1219 kJ/291 kcal
Protein 39 g/Carbs 5 g/Fat 13 g

CHICKEN TIKKA MASALA

This dish was most probably invented in British Indian restaurants, and is now a standard item on most menus. It is very popular as it's relatively mild – try with prawns, or with paneer or mixed vegetables for a vegetarian option.

INGREDIENTS

- 10 g fresh root ginger, peeled, cut in round slices (2 mm)
- 2 garlic cloves
- 1 tsp fine sea salt
- 50 g ghee
- 40 g onion, halved
- ¼ tsp ground turmeric
- ½ tsp ground cumin
- ½ tsp ground coriander
- ½ tsp garam masala
- 2 tsp paprika
- 1 tsp sugar, or to taste
- 1 Tbsp tomato purée
- 400 g tinned chopped tomatoes (1 x 400 g tin)
- 125 g water
- ½ chicken stock cube (for 0.5 l)
- 50 g whipping cream
- 25 g ground almonds
- 500 g cooked chicken tikka (see recipe, page 56)

PREPARATION

1. Place ginger, garlic and salt in mixing bowl then chop **5 sec/speed 5**. Transfer to a bowl and set aside.
2. Place ghee and onion in mixing bowl then chop **5 sec/speed 5**. Fry **5 min/Varoma/speed ⟲**.
3. Add reserved chopped ginger and garlic then fry **1 min 30 sec/100°C/speed ⟲**.
4. Add turmeric, cumin, coriander, garam masala, paprika, sugar and tomato purée then cook **2 min/100°C/speed ⟲**.
5. Add tinned tomatoes, water and stock cube then cook **15 min/100°C/speed 1**.
6. Add cream and ground almonds then blend **30 sec/speed 9**.
7. Add cooked chicken tikka pieces and heat **10 min/95°C/⟲/speed 0.5**. Serve with rice or naan bread.

10 min

45 min

easy

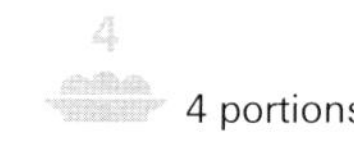
4 portions

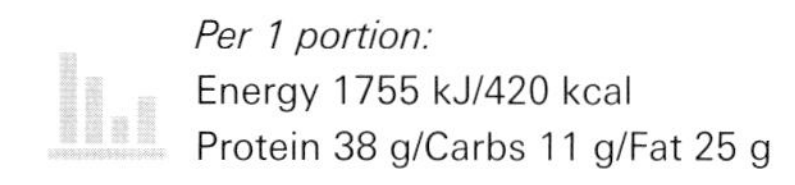
Per 1 portion:
Energy 1755 kJ/420 kcal
Protein 38 g/Carbs 11 g/Fat 25 g

CHICKEN AKHNI

This aromatic, flavourful one-pot rice dish is a pilau that has its roots in East Africa. This is the perfect meal to serve if you have several mouths to feed; baked in the oven for an hour you can simply bring the dish straight to the table. It is a hearty meal on cold winter nights and can be eaten with a raita (page 130) and/or pickle or just as is.

INGREDIENTS

- 50 g vegetable oil, plus extra for greasing
- 350 g basmati rice, washed and drained
- 700 g water, boiling
- 100 g onions, quartered
- 25 g fresh root ginger, peeled, cut in round slices (2 mm)
- 2 garlic cloves
- 3 dried Kashmiri chillies
- 4 whole cloves
- 1 cinnamon stick
- 4 cardamom pods
- 6 black peppercorns
- 1 tsp cumin seeds
- 500 g chicken thighs, boneless and skinless, diced (2.5 cm)
- 150 g ripe tomatoes, quartered
- 120 g plain yoghurt
- 2 tsp fine sea salt
- 1 small handful fresh coriander leaves, chopped, for garnish (approx. 5 g)

USEFUL ITEMS

- large baking dish (approx. 26 cm x 24 cm x 5 cm)
- aluminium foil

PREPARATION

1. Grease a large baking dish (approx. 26 cm x 24 cm x 5 cm). Add rice and boiling water to baking dish then set aside.
2. Place oil in mixing bowl and heat **1 min/Varoma/speed** .
3. Add onions, ginger, garlic and chillies then chop **10 sec/speed 5**. Scrape down sides of mixing bowl with spatula then, without measuring cup, fry **7 min/Varoma/speed** .
4. Add cloves, cinnamon, cardamom, peppercorns and cumin seeds then, with measuring cup, cook **2 min/Varoma/speed** . Meanwhile, preheat oven to 180°C.
5. Add chicken, tomatoes, yoghurt and salt then cook **10 min/100°C/⟲/speed 1**. Pour mixture over reserved soaked rice and stir well with spatula. Cover dish tightly with aluminium foil. Bake for 1 hour (180°C) until rice and chicken are cooked. Serve garnished with coriander leaves.

10 min

1 hour 30 min

easy

6 portions

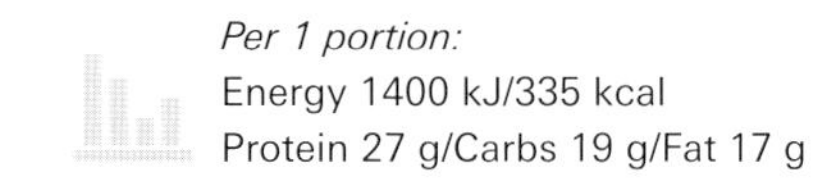
Per 1 portion:
Energy 1400 kJ/335 kcal
Protein 27 g/Carbs 19 g/Fat 17 g

CHICKEN SAAG

This traditional, leafy ('saag' means 'leafy green vegetables') north Indian dish is a protein-packed feast of chicken and spinach. Serve with rice and bread. You can substitute chicken with paneer for a vegetarian version.

INGREDIENTS

1 tsp coriander seeds
1 tsp cumin seeds
1 tsp fenugreek seeds
700 g fresh spinach leaves
20 g fresh root ginger, peeled, cut in round slices (2 mm)
100 g onions, quartered
3 garlic cloves
1 fresh red chilli, halved, deseeded (optional)
20 g vegetable oil
1 tsp garam masala
1 tsp ground turmeric
50 g plum tomatoes, halved
10 g fresh coriander
150 g water
1 chicken stock cube (for 0.5 l)
1 tsp fine sea salt
700 g chicken breasts, skinless, diced (3 cm)
150 g plain yoghurt
30 g lemon juice

PREPARATION

1. Place coriander, cumin and fenugreek seeds in mixing bowl then toast **5 min/Varoma/speed 0.5**. Grind **2 min/speed 9**. Transfer to a bowl and set aside.
2. Place 350 g spinach in mixing bowl and chop **15 sec/speed 5** while stirring with spatula through hole in mixing bowl lid. Cook **3 min/100°C/speed 1**.
3. Add remaining 350 g spinach and chop **20 sec/speed 5** while stirring with spatula through hole in mixing bowl lid. Cook **5 min/100°C/speed 2**. Drain using simmering basket, discarding liquid and set cooked spinach aside.
4. Place ginger, onions, garlic and chilli (if using) in mixing bowl then chop **4 sec/speed 6**. Scrape down sides of mixing bowl with spatula then chop again **2 sec/speed 6**.
5. Add oil, garam masala, turmeric and reserved ground spices then sauté **4 min/100°C/speed 1**.
6. Add tomatoes, fresh coriander, water, stock cube, salt and half the reserved chopped spinach then blend **1 min/speed 8**.
7. Add chicken and remaining reserved chopped spinach then cook **12 min/100°C/↺/speed 1**.
8. Add 100 g yoghurt and lemon juice then stir in with spatula. Serve warm, drizzled with remaining 50 g yoghurt, with rice or Indian bread.

VARIATION

- Use frozen chopped spinach, thawed and drained, instead of fresh spinach.

20 min

50 min

easy

6 portions
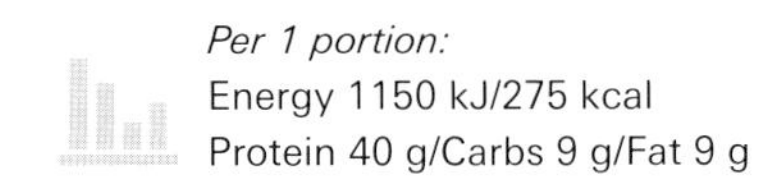
Per 1 portion:
Energy 1150 kJ/275 kcal
Protein 40 g/Carbs 9 g/Fat 9 g

BUTTER CHICKEN

This dish is popular with fans of milder curries. As the name indicates, it is made with butter or ghee. This simplified Thermomix® version is quick to make so ideal for a weekday meal, served with rice or naan.

INGREDIENTS

500 g chicken breasts, skinless, diced (2-3 cm)
100 g tikka paste (see page 24)
40 g ghee
150 g onions, quartered
20 g fresh root ginger, peeled, cut in round slices (2 mm)
10 g fresh coriander
3 garlic cloves
2 fresh green chillies, halved, deseeded if desired
1 tsp fine sea salt
2 tsp ground cumin
2 tsp ground coriander
½ tsp ground turmeric
100 g water
70 g tomato purée
500 g single cream

PREPARATION

1. Place a large bowl on mixing bowl lid and weigh in chicken and Tikka paste. Remove bowl from lid, stir well then set aside.
2. Place ghee in mixing bowl and heat **1 min/Varoma/speed 1**.
3. Add onions, ginger, fresh coriander, garlic and chillies then mince **10 sec/speed 5**. Scrape down sides of mixing bowl with spatula then, replace measuring cup with simmering basket, and fry **5 min/Varoma/speed 2**.
4. Add salt, cumin, coriander and turmeric then, with measuring cup in place, fry **3 min/Varoma/speed 2**.
5. Add water and cook **5 min/Varoma/speed 1**.
6. Add reserved marinated chicken, tomato purée and cream then cook **20 min/100°C/⟲/speed [soft]**. Serve hot with rice or Indian bread to soak up the sauce.

TIPS

- Butter chicken is often served as part of a banquet meal.
- The chicken can be left to marinate overnight, at end of step 1, for even more depth of flavour.

15 min

50 min

easy

4 portions

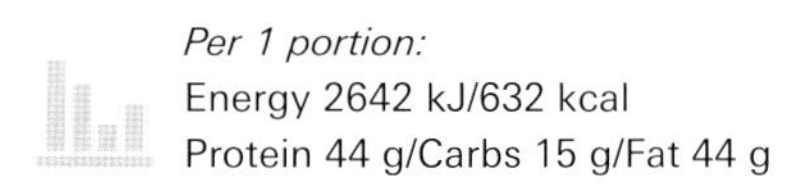
Per 1 portion:
Energy 2642 kJ/632 kcal
Protein 44 g/Carbs 15 g/Fat 44 g

CHICKEN AND MUSHROOM BALTI

This literally translated, in Urdu, means 'chicken and mushroom wok'. This type of Indian stir-fry cooking in a metal wok is thought to have originated in Pakistan. Balti is an aromatic and herby curry, and one of the most popular in the UK and Ireland. One of the benefits of this recipe is that once the balti paste is made, you can enjoy your curry in minutes! Add other vegetables of your choice for a variation to this recipe.

INGREDIENTS

Balti Paste

280 g fresh coriander, leaves and stalks
2 fresh red chillies, halved, deseeded
15 garlic cloves
40 g fresh root ginger, peeled, cut in round slices (2 mm)
150 g onions, quartered
60 g vegetable oil or ghee
3 Tbsp ground coriander
1 tsp ground cumin
½ tsp ground turmeric
120 g tinned tomatoes
1½ tsp fine sea salt
½ tsp sugar
2 tsp garam masala
120 g water

Curry

1 Tbsp vegetable oil, for frying
1 Tbsp cumin seeds
½ chicken stock cube (for 0.5 l)
150 g water, hot
500 g chicken breasts, skinless, sliced (2 cm)
50 g onions, sliced (1 cm)
70 g red peppers, diced (2 cm)
1-2 fresh green chillies, sliced (1 cm), to taste
200 g button mushrooms, sliced (5 mm)
1 tsp lemon juice, or to taste

PREPARATION

Balti Paste

1. Place 140 g fresh coriander in mixing bowl and chop **5 sec/speed 8**. Transfer to a bowl and set aside.
2. Place chillies, garlic, ginger and remaining 140 g fresh coriander in mixing bowl then chop **5 sec/speed 8**.
3. Add onions and oil then chop **5 sec/speed 5**. Scrape down sides of mixing bowl with spatula.
4. Add ground coriander, cumin and turmeric then sauté **7 min/100°C/speed 1**.
5. Add tomatoes, salt, sugar and garam masala then chop **20 sec/speed 7**. Scrape down sides and lid of mixing bowl with spatula.
6. Add water and cook **6 min/Varoma/speed**.
7. Add reserved chopped coriander and stir **15 sec/speed**. Transfer to sterilised jars, seal and label then set aside.

Continued on page **68** ▶

35 min

50 min

easy

4 portions

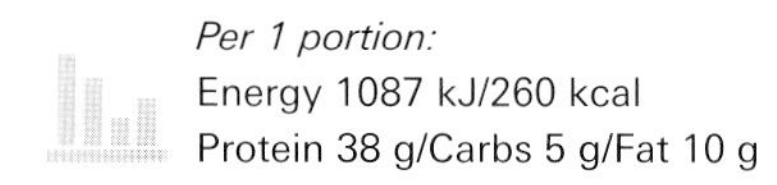
Per 1 portion:
Energy 1087 kJ/260 kcal
Protein 38 g/Carbs 5 g/Fat 10 g

▶ CHICKEN AND MUSHROOM BALTI, continued

USEFUL ITEMS

sterilised jam jars
deep frying pan

Curry

8. Heat oil and cumin seeds in a large frying pan over a medium-high heat.
9. Add 4 Tbsp balti paste and stir fry for 1 minute. Meanwhile, dissolve stock cube in hot water.
10. Add chicken pieces and stir fry for 10-12 minutes while gradually adding 100 g prepared chicken stock.
11. Add onions, red peppers, chillies, mushrooms and remaining 50 g stock then simmer for 5 minutes until chicken is cooked. Stir in lemon juice then serve.

TIP

- The recipe for balti paste makes more than is needed for this recipe (approx. 600 g total). Store the remainder in sterilised, airtight jars in the fridge for up to 2 weeks or in the freezer for up to a month.

VARIATION

- Diced vegetables, diced paneer, or prawns can be used in place of chicken.

PULLED TANDOORI CHICKEN

This modern take on tandoori chicken features shredding the meat for use in breads as a snack, or as part of a larger meal. It can also be served cold.

INGREDIENTS

Chicken

1 garlic clove
40 g red onion, halved
10 g fresh root ginger, peeled, cut in round slices (2 mm)
800 g water
1 chicken stock cube (for 0.5 l)
600 g chicken breasts, skinless, sliced (3 cm)

Sauce

200 g coconut milk

1 tsp paprika
1 tsp ground cumin
1 tsp ground turmeric
1 tsp garam masala
½ tsp Kashmiri chilli powder
½ tsp fine sea salt

USEFUL ITEMS

serving bowl with lid

PREPARATION

Chicken

1. Place garlic, onion and ginger in mixing bowl then chop **5 sec/speed 5**. Scrape down sides of mixing bowl with spatula.
2. Add water and stock cube then heat **6 min/100°C/speed 1**.
3. Add chicken and simmer **12 min/98°C/↺/speed 🥄**. Drain using simmering basket and discard cooking liquid.
4. Return chicken to mixing bowl and shred **4 sec/↺/speed 4**. Transfer to a serving bowl, cover and keep warm.

Sauce

5. Place all sauce ingredients in mixing bowl and mix **10 sec/speed 3**. Pour over chicken and stir well. Serve immediately, or enjoy cold.

TIP

- If eating cold, the chicken and sauce can be kept separately in the fridge then mixed together just before serving.

 10 min
 30 min
 easy
6 portions
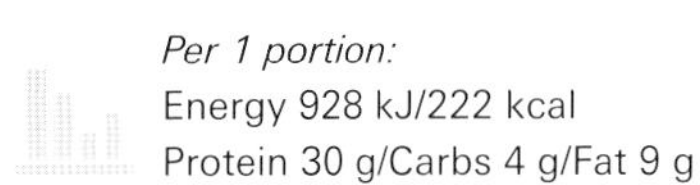
Per 1 portion:
Energy 928 kJ/222 kcal
Protein 30 g/Carbs 4 g/Fat 9 g

CHICKEN JALFREZI

A traditional jalfrezi involves frying the meat ('frezi' means stir-fry), but the results are just as impressive and healthier when prepared in your Thermomix®. In the days of the Raj, Bengali chefs often cooked this dish using leftover cooked meat or poultry. Just as delicious prepared as a vegetable curry, too.

INGREDIENTS

Marinade
450 g chicken breasts, skinless, cut in pieces (3 cm)
2 tsp ground coriander
2 tsp ground cumin
2 tsp ground turmeric

Tomato Sauce
20 g vegetable oil
50 g onions, quartered
2 garlic cloves
1 fresh green chilli, halved
400 g tinned chopped tomatoes (1 x 400 g tin)
250 g water
1 tsp ground coriander
1 tsp ground cumin
1 tsp ground turmeric
1 tsp fine sea salt

Curry
20 g vegetable oil
120 g onions, quartered
250 g red peppers, diced (2-3 cm)
2 fresh red chillies, halved
1 tsp garam masala
10 g fresh coriander leaves, chopped

USEFUL ITEMS
cling film

PREPARATION

Marinade
1. Place a bowl on mixing bowl lid and weigh in chicken. Remove bowl from lid, add ground coriander, cumin and turmeric then stir well. Cover with cling film and set aside in fridge to marinate while making tomato sauce.

Tomato Sauce
2. Place oil, onions, garlic and green chilli in mixing bowl then chop **5 sec/speed 5**. Scrape down sides of mixing bowl with spatula then sauté **5 min/120°C/speed** .
3. Add tomatoes, water, ground coriander, cumin, turmeric and salt then blend **30 sec/speed 8**. Scrape down sides and lid of mixing bowl with spatula then simmer **15 min/98°C/speed 0.5**. Transfer to a bowl and set aside. Rinse mixing bowl.

Curry
4. Place oil and onions in mixing bowl then chop **2 sec/speed 5**.
5. Add diced peppers and chillies then cook **10 min/100°C/ /speed** .
6. Add marinated chicken and reserved tomato sauce then cook **15 min/100°C/ /speed** . Stir in garam masala and chopped coriander leaves then serve with pilau rice or Indian bread.

TIP
- The chicken can be left to marinate overnight for an even greater depth of flavour.

 15 min  1 hour  easy 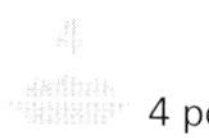 4 portions 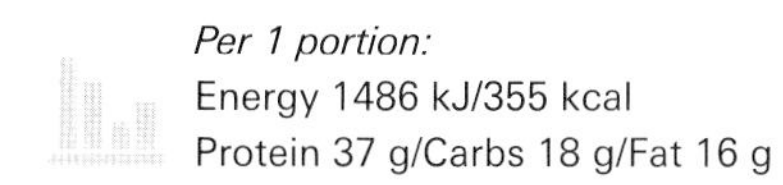

Per 1 portion:
Energy 1486 kJ/355 kcal
Protein 37 g/Carbs 18 g/Fat 16 g

QUICK LAMB DHANSAK

This popular Parsi dish of lamb and lentils contains varying amounts of sugar, tamarind and chilli for sweet, sour and hot tastes. Dhansak is a rich dish, and traditionally one for a weekend meal as its slow cook can take several hours. This quick version, which is every bit as flavoursome, is ready in 50 minutes making it suitable for all occasions.

INGREDIENTS

5 g fresh mint leaves
5 g fresh coriander leaves
500 g lamb, lean, diced (2-3 cm)
2 Tbsp garam masala
30 g vegetable oil, plus 2 Tbsp for frying
150 g onions, quartered
2 garlic cloves
200 g butternut squash, peeled, diced (2-3 cm)
150 g red split lentils, rinsed
20 g rogan josh curry paste (or other Indian curry paste)
15 g tamarind paste
25 g caster sugar
500 g water, hot
1 vegetable stock cube (for 0.5 l)
½ tsp fine sea salt, or to taste
¼ tsp ground black pepper, or to taste
30 g lemon juice

USEFUL ITEMS

large bowl
frying pan

PREPARATION

1. Place mint and coriander leaves in mixing bowl then chop **3 sec/speed 5**. Transfer to a small bowl and set aside.
2. Place a large bowl on mixing bowl lid and weigh in lamb. Remove bowl from lid and add garam masala then stir well.
3. Heat 2 Tbsp oil in a frying pan over a high heat. Fry lamb in batches for 2-3 minutes until browned all over. Transfer to a plate and set aside.
4. Place onions and garlic in mixing bowl then chop **5 sec/speed 5**. Scrape down sides of mixing bowl with spatula.
5. Add 30 g oil and butternut squash then cook **8 min/100°C/↺/speed 🥄**.
6. Add lentils, curry paste, tamarind paste, sugar, hot water, stock cube and reserved lamb and juices then, without measuring cup, cook **30 min/98°C/↺/speed 🥄**.
7. Add salt, pepper, reserved chopped herbs and lemon juice then stir well with spatula. Adjust seasoning if desired, then serve with your choice of rice, Indian bread and side dishes.

15 min  50 min  easy 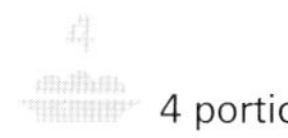 4 portions

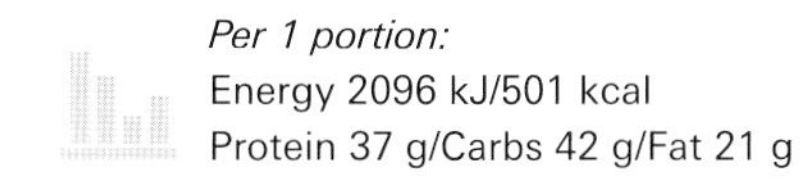
Per 1 portion:
Energy 2096 kJ/501 kcal
Protein 37 g/Carbs 42 g/Fat 21 g

KOFTA CURRY

The name 'kofta' comes from the Arabic for 'meatballs' and they take different shapes, sizes and names in many cuisines around the world. Koftas can be served as a starter or a main dish, either dry or as here, made into a curry. They can be made from many different meats including lamb, beef and chicken or even seafood.

INGREDIENTS

Koftas

120 g onions, quartered
30 g fresh coriander leaves
25 g fresh root ginger, peeled, cut in round slices (2 mm)
2 fresh green chillies, halved, deseeded
4 garlic cloves
1 tsp coriander seeds (optional)
1 tsp fine sea salt
½ tsp ground black pepper, or to taste
500 g beef mince or lamb mince, broken in pieces
1 tsp lemon juice

Sauce

30 g ghee
1 tsp garlic powder
1 tsp ground turmeric
1 tsp garam masala
1 tsp fenugreek leaves, dried
¼ tsp asafoetida
¼ tsp caraway seeds
80 g onions, quartered
500 g passata
80 g water

USEFUL ITEMS

cling film
serving bowl

PREPARATION

Koftas

1. Place onions, fresh coriander, ginger, chillies, garlic, coriander seeds (if using), salt and pepper in mixing bowl then chop **5 sec/speed 6**. Scrape down sides of bowl with spatula.
2. Add mince and lemon juice then mix **20 sec/↺/speed 2**. Scrape down sides of mixing bowl with spatula then mix again **20 sec/↺/speed 2**.
3. Using wet hands, shape mixture into 24 small meatballs (koftas) then place on a large plate. Cover and set aside in fridge. Meanwhile, clean mixing bowl and prepare sauce.

Sauce

4. Place ghee in mixing bowl and heat **2 min/100°C/speed 🥄**.
5. Add garlic powder, turmeric, garam masala, fenugreek leaves, asafoetida and caraway seeds then fry **1 min 30 sec/100°C/speed 1**.
6. Add onions and chop **3 sec/speed 5**. Scrape down sides of mixing bowl with spatula then sauté **2 min/120°C/speed 1**.
7. Add passata and water. Place koftas in Varoma dish then place Varoma into position and cook **40 min/Varoma/speed 1**. Transfer koftas to a serving bowl and pour sauce over. Mix well then serve with rice or Indian bread.

VARIATIONS

- For added texture, instead of steaming, the koftas can be fried in a little oil until cooked and browned on all sides. Alternatively, cook under a hot grill.
- The koftas can also be served on their own without sauce – great for a picnic, or as a canapé or starter.

25 min

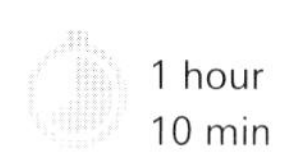
1 hour 10 min

easy

4 portions

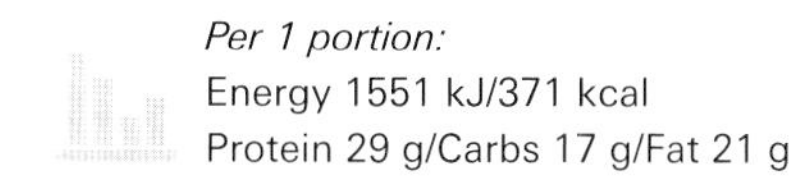
Per 1 portion:
Energy 1551 kJ/371 kcal
Protein 29 g/Carbs 17 g/Fat 21 g

LAMB ROGAN JOSH

Rogan josh, said to originate from Kashmir in Moghul times, is traditionally made with fatty meat ('rogan' means 'fat') with intense flavours ('josh' translates as 'intense'). However, many adaptations exist and more lean meat is preferred nowadays.

INGREDIENTS

8 garlic cloves
20 g fresh root ginger, peeled, cut in round slices (2 mm)
260 g water
20 g vegetable oil, plus 2 Tbsp for frying
1000 g lamb shoulder or leg, boneless, diced (2-3 cm)
10 cardamom pods
2 dried bay leaves
6 cloves
10 black peppercorns
¼ cinnamon stick
200 g onions, quartered
1 tsp ground coriander
2 tsp ground cumin
4 tsp paprika
¼-1 tsp ground cayenne pepper, to taste
1¼ tsp fine sea salt
100 g plain yoghurt
1 tsp garam masala, for garnish
½ tsp ground black pepper, for garnish
3 sprigs fresh coriander, leaves only, chopped, for garnish

USEFUL ITEMS

frying pan

PREPARATION

1. Place garlic, ginger, and 60 g water in mixing bowl then blend **10 sec/speed 10**. Transfer to a bowl and set aside.
2. Heat 2 Tbsp oil in a large frying pan over a high heat. Fry lamb in batches for 2-3 minutes until browned all over. Transfer to a bowl and set aside.
3. Place cardamon, bay leaves, cloves, peppercorns and cinnamon stick in a hot frying pan and toast for 1-2 minutes until cloves swell and bay leaves begin to colour. Remove from heat.
4. Place 20 g oil and onions in mixing bowl then chop **5 sec/speed 5**. Scrape down sides of mixing bowl with spatula then sauté **6 min/120°C/speed**.
5. Add reserved garlic ginger paste, ground coriander, cumin, paprika, cayenne, salt and reserved toasted spices then sauté **1 min 30 sec/100°C//speed**.
6. Add reserved browned lamb with juices and yoghurt then cook **3 min/98°C//speed**.
7. Add remaining 200 g water then, replace measuring cup with simmering basket, and cook **60 min/100°C//speed**.
8. With simmering basket still in place, reduce **15 min/105°C//speed**. Serve hot, sprinkled with garam masala, ground black pepper and chopped coriander leaves.

VARIATION

- Stewing steak can be used instead of lamb. Add an extra 140 g water (total 340 g) at step 7 and proceed with recipe.

15 min

1 hour 45 min

easy

6 portions

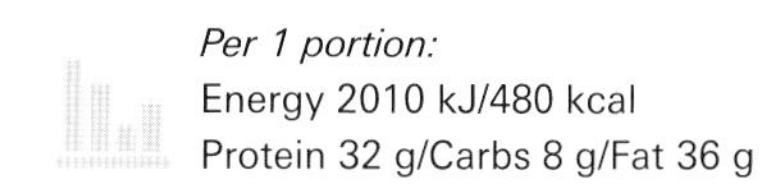
Per 1 portion:
Energy 2010 kJ/480 kcal
Protein 32 g/Carbs 8 g/Fat 36 g

LAMB KEEMA WITH PEAS 

This quick, tasty, low-budget dish makes an excellent midweek option. It's an incredibly versatile dish that can be used as a starter, snack or main course. It's often sold as street food in India, where it is cooked on a tawa, a large iron griddle, and eaten with pau (bread).

INGREDIENTS

2 Tbsp cumin seeds
1 Tbsp coriander seeds
15 g fresh root ginger, peeled, cut in round slices (2 mm)
5 garlic cloves
1-2 fresh bird's eye chillies, halved, to taste
150 g onions, quartered
30 g ghee ☞
6 cloves
1 cinnamon stick, small
6 black peppercorns
1 tsp ground turmeric
1 Tbsp garam masala ☞, or to taste
500 g lamb mince, broken in pieces
400 g tinned chopped tomatoes (1 x 400 g tin)
200 g water
½ meat stock cube (for 0.5 l), lamb or beef
2 tsp fine sea salt, or to taste
150 g frozen green peas

PREPARATION

1. Place cumin and coriander seeds in mixing bowl then toast **8 min/Varoma/speed 🥄**. Grind **2 min/speed 10.** Transfer to a bowl and set aside.
2. Place ginger, garlic and chillies in mixing bowl then chop **3 sec/speed 6**. Transfer to a bowl and set aside.
3. Place onions and ghee in mixing bowl then chop **5 sec/speed 5**. Scrape down sides of mixing bowl with spatula.
4. Add cloves, cinnamon and peppercorns then sauté **7 min/100°C/↺/speed 0.5**. Remove and discard cinnamon stick.
5. Add turmeric, garam masala and 1 Tbsp reserved ground cumin and coriander then fry **1 min/100°C/speed 🥄**.
6. Add lamb mince and cook **3 min/100°C/↺/speed 0.5**.
7. Add tomatoes, water, stock cube, salt and reserved chopped garlic mixture then simmer **20 min/95°C/↺/speed 🥄**.
8. Add peas and cook **5 min/98°C/↺/speed 🥄**. Check seasoning and add more salt or garam masala if desired. Serve with rice or chapatis.

TIP

- Drained of liquid, this keema makes a good meat filling option for samosas – see page 36.

VARIATION

- Use 500 g leftover roast lamb instead of lamb mince to make this curry. Add lamb, in pieces (2 cm), at step 7.

 15 min  1 hour  easy 

4 portions 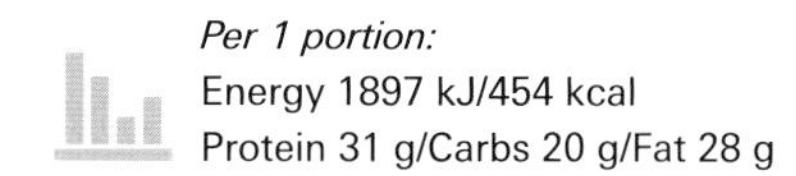

Per 1 portion:
Energy 1897 kJ/454 kcal
Protein 31 g/Carbs 20 g/Fat 28 g

BEEF MADRAS

Madras curry is thought to have originated in Madras (now Chennai) in South India, when it was probably a variation of a rich vegetarian curry. Our madras uses beef, and while this wouldn't be done in India where the cow is a sacred animal, it is a very popular combination in curry houses here.

INGREDIENTS

10 g fresh root ginger, peeled, cut in round slices (2 mm)
2 garlic cloves
100 g onions, quartered
4 Tbsp vegetable oil
600 g braising steak, diced (2 cm)
2 Tbsp madras curry powder
50 g tomato purée
300 g water, or enough to cover meat
½ beef stock cube (for 0.5 l)
2 Tbsp lemon juice

USEFUL ITEMS

frying pan

PREPARATION

1. Place ginger and garlic in mixing bowl then chop **3 sec/speed 7**. Transfer to a bowl and set aside.
2. Place onions and 2 Tbsp oil in mixing bowl then chop **5 sec/speed 5**. Scrape down sides of mixing bowl with spatula then sauté **8 min/120°C/speed**. Meanwhile, heat remaining 2 Tbsp oil in a large frying pan over a high heat. Fry beef in batches for 2-3 minutes until browned all over. Transfer to a bowl and set aside.
3. Add madras curry powder and reserved chopped ginger and garlic then fry **1 min 30 sec/100°C/speed**.
4. Add reserved browned beef and juices, tomato purée, water and stock cube then, replace measuring cup with simmering basket, and simmer **60 min/98°C/↺/speed**. With simmering basket still in place, reduce **10 min/105°C/↺/speed**.
5. Add lemon juice and stir in with spatula. Serve with pilau or cumin rice and poppadoms.

TIP

- This curry can be made hotter by adding 1 or 2 halved fresh chillies in step 1.

15 min

1 hour 30 min

easy

6 portions

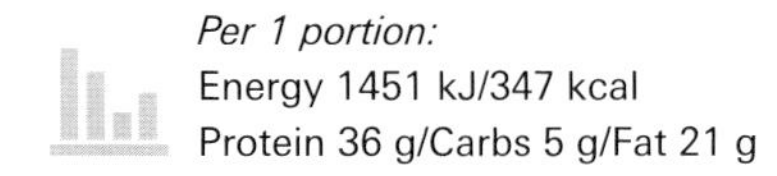

Per 1 portion:
Energy 1451 kJ/347 kcal
Protein 36 g/Carbs 5 g/Fat 21 g

PORK VINDALOO

This hot and fiery dish has its roots in the Portuguese-speaking part of India, Goa. As such, the name (in Portuguese) indicates vinegar and garlic, and uses chillies that were introduced to Goa by the Portuguese. It also uses garam masala which adds further heat. Though we have made it here with the authentic pork, it often uses chicken or lamb so feel free to substitute it with a meat of your choice.

INGREDIENTS

Marinade
800 g pork shoulder, boneless, diced (2 cm)
5 cardamom pods
5 cloves
4 fresh red chillies, halved
1 cinnamon stick
1 tsp black peppercorns
1 tsp coriander seeds
½ tsp fenugreek seeds
30 g white wine vinegar
15 g red wine vinegar
1 Tbsp fine sea salt
½ tsp ground turmeric

Curry
30 g vegetable oil
200 g onions, quartered
5 garlic cloves
15 g fresh root ginger, peeled, cut in round slices (2 mm)
250 g ripe tomatoes, quartered
2-6 fresh bird's eye chillies, halved, to taste
1 tsp brown sugar
80 g water
5 g fresh coriander leaves, chopped

USEFUL ITEMS
cling film
serving bowl

PREPARATION

Marinade
1. Place a bowl on mixing bowl lid and weigh in pork then set bowl aside.
2. Place cardamom pods, cloves, red chillies, cinnamon stick, peppercorns, coriander seeds and fenugreek seeds in mixing bowl then grind **2 min/speed 10**. Scrape down sides of mixing bowl with spatula.
3. Add white wine vinegar, red wine vinegar, salt and turmeric then mix **15 sec/speed 9**. Pour over pork and stir well. Cover and set aside in fridge to marinate for at least 3 hours or overnight. Clean mixing bowl.

Curry
4. Place oil, onions and garlic in mixing bowl then chop **5 sec/speed 5**. Sauté **5 min/Varoma/speed 1**.
5. Add ginger, tomatoes, chillies and sugar then mix **20 sec/speed 5**.
6. Add reserved marinated pork and water then cook **45 min/100°C/↺/speed 🥄**. Transfer to a serving bowl, sprinkle with chopped fresh coriander and serve with rice or naan breads.

TIPS
- Serve with yoghurt or raita on the side to counteract the heat from the curry.
- The pork can be left to marinate overnight for even greater depth of flavour.

10 min

4 hour

easy

6 portions

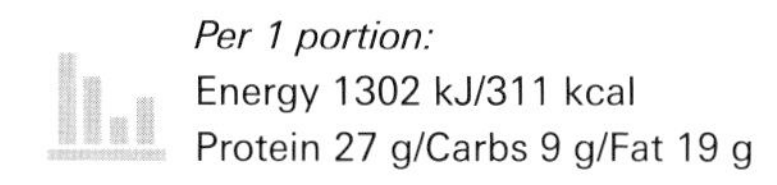
Per 1 portion:
Energy 1302 kJ/311 kcal
Protein 27 g/Carbs 9 g/Fat 19 g

JUNGLI LAAL MAAS

This fiery curry originated in Rajasthan. 'Jungli' means 'wild' and traditionally this dish was prepared with game meat such as wild boar. The long cooking time means it is a dish that also suits tougher meats such as mutton. 'Laal' means 'red' and here it refers to the red meat as well as the red chillies.

INGREDIENTS

Marinade

600 g venison, diced (2-3 cm)
200 g plain yoghurt
3 Tbsp red chilli paste
1 tsp fine sea salt
4 garlic cloves
15 g fresh root ginger, peeled, cut in round slices (2 mm)

Curry

5 dried Kashmiri chillies
1½ Tbsp coriander seeds
¾ tsp cumin seeds
200 g onions, quartered
20 g ghee
1 cinnamon stick, small
5 green cardamom pods
3 black cardamom pods
2 bay leaves
10 garlic cloves
250 g water

USEFUL ITEMS

cling film
large bowl

PREPARATION

Marinade

1. Place a bowl on mixing bowl lid and weigh in venison and yoghurt. Remove bowl, add red chilli paste and salt then set bowl aside.
2. Place 4 garlic cloves and ginger in mixing bowl then chop **3 sec/speed 7**. Add to bowl with meat and stir well with spatula. Cover and set aside in fridge to marinate for at least 3 hours or overnight. Clean mixing bowl.

Curry

3. Place dried Kashmiri chillies, coriander seeds and cumin seeds in mixing bowl then grind **2 min/speed 10**. Transfer to a bowl and set aside.
4. Place onions in mixing bowl and chop **5 sec/speed 5**. Transfer to a bowl and set aside.
5. Place ghee, cinnamon stick, green cardamom and black cardamom pods in mixing bowl then fry **5 min/Varoma/⟲/speed 🥄**.
6. Add bay leaves and reserved chopped onions then fry **6 min/120°C/⟲/speed 🥄**.
7. Add 10 garlic cloves and reserved ground spices then fry **3 min/120°C/⟲/speed 🥄**.
8. Add reserved marinated venison and fry **4 min/120°C/⟲/speed 0.5**.
9. Add water and stir well with spatula. Cook **75-90 min/98°C/⟲/speed 🥄** until meat is tender. Adjust seasoning if necessary and serve.

TIP

- The venison can be left to marinate overnight for even greater depth of flavour.

15 min

5 hour

easy

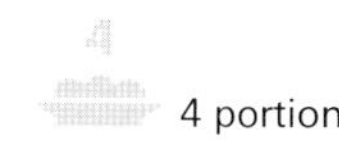
4 portions

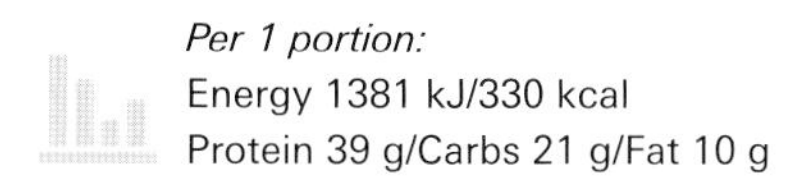
Per 1 portion:
Energy 1381 kJ/330 kcal
Protein 39 g/Carbs 21 g/Fat 10 g

MAINS – FISH AND SEAFOOD

KERALAN FISH CURRY

Down to the southern coast for this beautifully vibrant fish 'molee' (a stew typically cooked in coconut). The coconut offsets the light spice in this flaky fish curry, and the amount of heat can be altered by increasing or decreasing the number of chillies used.

INGREDIENTS

140 g onions, quartered
80 g vegetable oil
20 g fresh root ginger, peeled, cut in round slices (2 mm)
4 garlic cloves
2 fresh green chillies, halved, deseeded if desired
2 black cardamom pods, lightly crushed
4 cloves
1 cinnamon stick
1 tsp ground turmeric
1 tsp plain flour
1 tsp fine sea salt
600 g river cobbler fillets, skinless, cut in pieces (3-4 cm)
160 g coconut cream
90 g water
25 g lime juice

PREPARATION

1. Place onions, oil, ginger, garlic and chillies in mixing bowl then chop **5 sec/speed 5**. Scrape down sides of mixing bowl with spatula then sauté **8 min/Varoma/speed 0.5**.
2. Add black cardamom pods, cloves, cinnamon stick and turmeric then fry **2 min/100°C/speed 0.5**.
3. Add flour and salt then cook **1 min/100°C/speed 0.5**.
4. Add fish, coconut cream and water then simmer **5 min/98°C/↺/speed 🥄**.
5. Add lime juice and heat **2 min/98°C/↺/speed 🥄**. Remove cinnamon stick and serve warm.

VARIATION

- Instead of cobbler, use other thick, meaty white fish such as monkfish.

 10 min  30 min  easy  4 portions 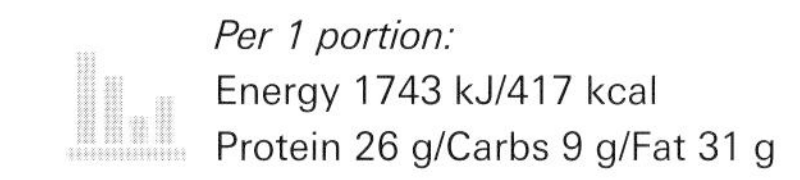

Per 1 portion:
Energy 1743 kJ/417 kcal
Protein 26 g/Carbs 9 g/Fat 31 g

PRAWN XACUTI

We go back to South India for this traditional curry. Pronounced 'shakooti', this dish has a unique flavour and aroma. The beautiful red colour comes from roasting the coconut and spices first.

INGREDIENTS

120 g desiccated coconut
2 Tbsp coriander seeds
2 tsp dried chilli flakes
1 tsp black peppercorns
1 tsp cumin seeds
1 tsp dried fennel seeds
1 cinnamon stick
4 cloves
2 star anise
1 Tbsp poppy seeds
440 g water
4 garlic cloves
200 g onions, quartered
25 g vegetable oil
1¼ tsp paprika
300-400 g peeled, raw prawns
½ tsp ground nutmeg
3 Tbsp tamarind paste
5 sprigs fresh coriander, leaves only, chopped, for garnish

USEFUL ITEMS

non-stick frying pan

PREPARATION

1. Spread desiccated coconut over a dry frying pan and toast over a low heat, stirring frequently, until golden brown. Transfer to a bowl and set aside.
2. Using the same frying pan, toast coriander seeds, dried chilli flakes, black peppercorns, cumin seeds, dried fennel seeds, cinnamon stick, cloves and star anise for 5 minutes.
3. Add poppy seeds and toast for a further 3 minutes, stirring occasionally. Transfer toasted spices to bowl with coconut and leave to cool for 15 minutes.
4. Place 45 g water, garlic and cooled toasted spices in mixing bowl then blend **30 sec/speed 9**. Scrape down sides of mixing bowl with spatula.
5. Add 45 g water and blend again **10 sec/speed 7** to a thick xacuti paste. Transfer to a bowl and set aside.
6. Place onions and oil in mixing bowl then chop **5 sec/speed 5**. Sauté **12 min/90°C/speed 0.5**.
7. Add reserved xacuti paste and fry **5 min/90°C/speed 0.5**.
8. Add paprika and 50 g water then cook **5 min/95°C/speed 0.5**.
9. Add remaining 300 g water and boil **3 min/100°C/speed 0.5**.
10. Add prawns and cook **3 min/95°C/⟲/speed 🥄**.
11. Add nutmeg and tamarind paste then simmer **5 min/90°C/⟲/speed 🥄**. Serve hot, sprinkled with chopped fresh coriander.

TIP

- For a thinner sauce, add an extra 50 g water in step 9.

20 min

1 hour 20 min

medium

4 portions

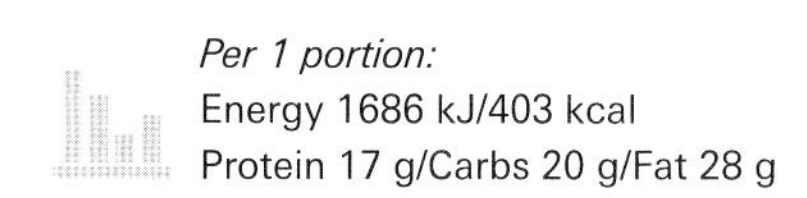
Per 1 portion:
Energy 1686 kJ/403 kcal
Protein 17 g/Carbs 20 g/Fat 28 g

TIMATAR WALI MACCHI (COD IN TOMATO SAUCE)

This deliciously aromatic dish produces mouth-wateringly flaky fish. It is a welcome variation from the heavier, highly spiced curry dishes and, served with rice it can be a complete meal.

INGREDIENTS

4 cod fillets, thick cut, skinless, boneless (approx. 120 g each)
1¼ tsp fine sea salt
½ tsp cayenne pepper
¼ tsp ground turmeric
50 g vegetable oil, plus 1-2 Tbsp for frying
1 tsp dried fennel seeds
1 tsp black mustard seeds
170 g onions, quartered
2 garlic cloves
400 g tinned chopped tomatoes (1 x 400 g tin)
2 tsp ground cumin
½ tsp garam masala

USEFUL ITEMS

deep sided baking dish
non-stick frying pan

PREPARATION

1. Place cod fillets on a plate and season with ¼ tsp salt, ¼ tsp cayenne pepper and ¼ tsp turmeric. Rub in well then set aside for 30 minutes while preparing sauce.
2. Place oil, fennel seeds and mustard seeds in mixing bowl then fry **5 min/120°C/speed 1**.
3. Add onions and garlic then chop **5 sec/speed 5**. Scrape down sides of mixing bowl with spatula then sauté **6 min/100°C/speed 1**. Meanwhile, preheat oven to 180°C.
4. Add tinned tomatoes, cumin, garam masala, remaining 1 tsp salt and remaining ¼ tsp cayenne pepper then cook **15 min/98°C/speed 0.5**. Towards the end of this time, heat 1-2 Tbsp oil in a frying pan over a high heat and lightly brown fish fillets for 1-2 minutes on each side.
5. Transfer browned fish fillets to a baking dish and pour over tomato sauce. Bake for 14-16 minutes (180°C) until fish is cooked. Serve immediately.

TIP

- Steam rice in the simmering basket while the fish is baking in the oven. There is no need to wash the mixing bowl as any residual sauce will only enhance the flavour of the rice.

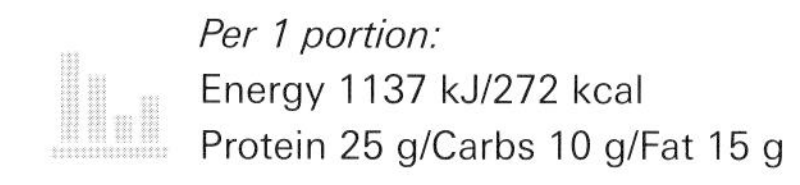

SEAFOOD KORMA

Korma has its roots in Moghul cuisine and can be traced back to the sixteenth century. Traditionally it is a dish where meat or vegetables are braised in water and stock, with yoghurt or cream added. One of the most popular milder Indian dishes, the heat can easily be adjusted to your taste, if desired.

INGREDIENTS

Garnish

10 g fresh coriander leaves
1 fresh green chilli, thinly sliced

Curry

60 g onions, quartered
60 g fresh tomatoes, quartered
60 g vegetable oil
15 g fresh root ginger, peeled, cut in round slices (2 mm)
3 garlic cloves
1 tsp ground cumin
1 tsp ground coriander
¼ tsp chilli powder
2 cloves
2 cardamom pods
20 g ground almonds
150 g coconut milk
150 g single cream
½ tsp fine sea salt
¼ tsp ground black pepper
30 g salted butter
100 g cod fillet, skinless, boneless, sliced (2 cm)
100 g raw squid rings
12 peeled, raw prawns, large

USEFUL ITEMS

frying pan

PREPARATION

Garnish

1. Place fresh coriander in mixing bowl and chop **3 sec/speed 8**. Transfer to a bowl then add sliced chilli and set bowl aside.

Curry

2. Place onions, tomatoes, 30 g oil, ginger and garlic in mixing bowl then chop **10 sec/speed 8**. Scrape down sides of mixing bowl with spatula.
3. Add cumin, ground coriander, chilli powder, cloves and cardamom pods then sauté **5 min/100°C/speed** .
4. Add ground almonds, coconut milk, cream, salt and pepper then simmer **8 min/98°C/speed 1**. Meanwhile, heat remaining 30 g oil and butter in a frying pan over a high heat, then sauté fish and seafood in batches to seal.
5. Add sealed fish, seafood and juices to mixing bowl then simmer **3 min/98°C/ /speed** until seafood is cooked. Serve immediately garnished with reserved chopped coriander and sliced chilli.

VARIATION

- Monkfish or scallops can be used instead of cod.

 15 min  40 min  easy  4 portions 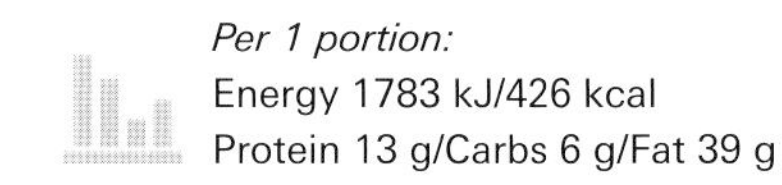

Per 1 portion:
Energy 1783 kJ/426 kcal
Protein 13 g/Carbs 6 g/Fat 39 g

DAHI WALI MACCHI (HADDOCK BAKED IN YOGHURT)

Another milder dish, and one great for entertaining as you can get most of the prep out of the way before the half hour baking time in the oven. Delicious served with pilau rice (see page 140) and vegetables.

INGREDIENTS

200 g onions, sliced (3 mm)
600 g haddock fillets, thick cut, skinless, boneless
10 g fresh root ginger, peeled, cut in round slices (2 mm)
425 g plain yoghurt
2 tsp ground cumin
1 tsp sugar
1½ tsp fine sea salt
½ tsp cayenne pepper
¼ tsp ground black pepper
¼ tsp garam masala
2 Tbsp ground coriander
2 Tbsp lemon juice
50 g vegetable oil
40 g butter
2 sprigs fresh coriander, leaves only, for garnish

USEFUL ITEMS

baking dish (approx. 22 cm x 30 cm)
aluminium foil

PREPARATION

1. Preheat oven to 190°C. Arrange sliced onions in a baking dish (large enough to contain fish in a single layer).
2. Cut fish fillets in 8 cm pieces. Place on top of onions in a single layer.
3. Place ginger in mixing bowl and chop **3 sec/speed 7**. Scrape down sides of mixing bowl with spatula. Chop again **3 sec/speed 7**.
4. Add yoghurt, cumin, sugar, salt, cayenne pepper, black pepper, garam masala, coriander and lemon juice then mix **15 sec/speed 3.5**.
5. Add oil and mix **15 sec/speed 4**. Pour over fish then cover dish with foil. Bake for 20-30 minutes (190°C) until fish is cooked. Meanwhile, clean mixing bowl.
6. When fish has cooked, carefully pour all cooking liquid into mixing bowl, leaving onions and fish in baking dish. Re-cover dish with foil to keep warm. Without measuring cup, reduce sauce **8 min/105°C/speed 0.5**.
7. Add butter and stir **1 min/speed 2**. Pour over cooked fish and serve immediately garnished with fresh coriander leaves.

15 min

50 min

easy

6 portions
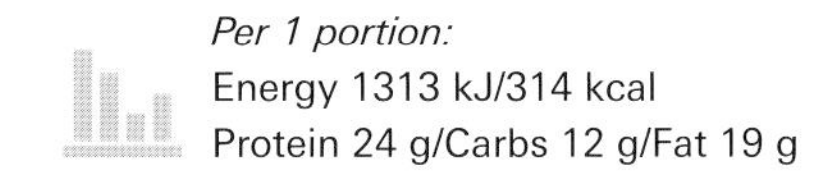
Per 1 portion:
Energy 1313 kJ/314 kcal
Protein 24 g/Carbs 12 g/Fat 19 g

PRAWN BHUNA

'Bhuna' is a method of cooking whereby spices are cooked over a high heat, adding liquid frequently to bring the temperature down and avoid burning the spices. However, in the Thermomix® spices can be cooked without catching, making this a very simple-to-make, tasty dish. In this recipe the mustard seeds are tempered first.

INGREDIENTS

20 g ghee
1 tsp black mustard seeds
50 g onions, quartered
1 garlic clove
1 tsp ground turmeric
1 tsp garam masala
½ tsp ground cumin
½ tsp ground coriander
½ tsp fine sea salt, or to taste
180 g tinned chopped tomatoes
40 g water
350 g peeled, raw prawns, large
5 sprigs fresh coriander,
leaves only, chopped (optional)

PREPARATION

1. Place ghee and mustard seeds in mixing bowl then fry **8 min/Varoma/speed**.
2. Add onions and garlic then chop **5 sec/speed 5**. Scrape down sides of mixing bowl with spatula then sauté **5 min/Varoma/speed**.
3. Add turmeric, garam masala, cumin, ground coriander, salt, tomatoes and water then cook **8 min/95°C/speed**.
4. Add prawns and cook **5 min/95°C//speed**. Serve sprinkled with chopped coriander leaves (if using), accompanied by dal or rice, or on puri for a prawn puri starter (see page 46).

5 min

30 min

easy

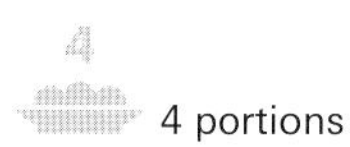

4 portions

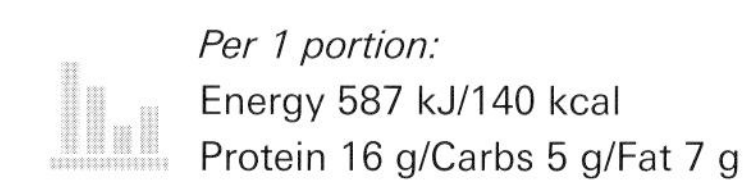

Per 1 portion:
Energy 587 kJ/140 kcal
Protein 16 g/Carbs 5 g/Fat 7 g

STEAMED SALMON PARCELS

If you were to create these Gujarati parcels authentically you'd wrap them in banana leaves, but greaseproof paper does the job just as well. The fish, encased in a fresh and zingy spice paste, will stay beautifully tender and moist by steaming as well as retain all the flavour of the marinade thanks to the paper parcels.

INGREDIENTS

Marinade
4 Tbsp lime juice (approx. 2½ limes)
1 tsp fine sea salt
½ tsp ground turmeric
4 fresh salmon fillets, thick cut, boneless (approx. 150 g each)

Spice Paste
60 g desiccated coconut
20 g fresh root ginger, peeled, cut in round slices (2 mm)
1 small handful fresh coriander leaves (approx. 5 g)
3 fresh green chillies, halved, deseeded if desired
2 garlic cloves
½ tsp cumin seeds, toasted
½ tsp sugar
¼ tsp ground turmeric
2 Tbsp vegetable oil

Rice
1200 g water
200 g basmati rice

USEFUL ITEMS
dish
greaseproof paper

PREPARATION

Marinade
1. Mix lime juice, salt and turmeric together in a large dish. Add salmon fillets and rub all over with marinade. Set aside for 15 minutes. Meanwhile, prepare spice paste.

Spice Paste
2. Place all spice paste ingredients in mixing bowl and blend **5 sec/speed 8**. Divide spice paste evenly between fish fillets in dish forming a layer on top. Cut four squares of greaseproof paper, large enough to wrap each fish fillet in. Place each fillet with spice paste on a square and wrap to form a parcel then place in Varoma dish.

Rice
3. Place water in mixing bowl. Insert simmering basket and weigh in rice. Rinse **10 sec/speed 5**.
4. Place covered Varoma into position and steam fish above rice **19 min/Varoma/speed 4**. Serve rice with salmon still in their parcels.

TIP
- Wear gloves when rubbing marinade into fish to avoid dyeing your hands with turmeric.

VARIATION
- Fresh coconut flesh can be used in place of desiccated coconut. Add fresh coconut, cut in pieces, with other spice paste ingredients and blend **15 sec/speed 8** in step 2.

 15 min  55 min  easy 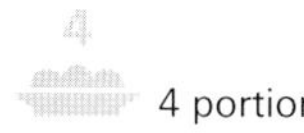 4 portions

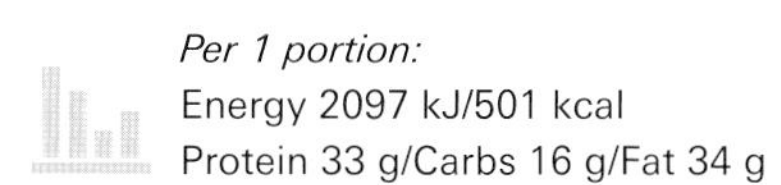

Per 1 portion:
Energy 2097 kJ/501 kcal
Protein 33 g/Carbs 16 g/Fat 34 g

MAINS – VEGETARIAN

PUDLA WITH SPINACH AND PANEER

Pudla are popular Indian chickpea pancakes or crêpes, which we've combined here with cheese and spinach for an Indian-French fusion dish! The pancakes are gluten-free and can be eaten as a snack or lunch – you could also serve the pudla alone with dal.

INGREDIENTS

Pudla

1 small handful fresh coriander leaves (approx. 5 g)
2 spring onions, cut in pieces (2 cm)
15 g fresh root ginger, peeled, cut in round slices (2 mm)
250 g water
200 g chickpea flour
1 tsp fine sea salt
1 tsp ground cumin
½ tsp ground turmeric

Filling

30 g vegetable oil, plus 2 tsp for frying
½ tsp cumin seeds
50 g onions, quartered
½ tsp ground cumin
½ tsp ground turmeric
½ tsp Kashmiri chilli powder
1 pinch ground nutmeg
1 garlic clove
150 g paneer cheese, cut in pieces
200 g fresh spinach leaves
150 g single cream
½ tsp fine sea salt, or to taste

USEFUL ITEMS

jug
ladle
pancake pan or frying pan

PREPARATION

Pudla

1. Place coriander, spring onions and ginger in mixing bowl then chop **3 sec/speed 7**. Scrape down sides of mixing bowl with spatula then chop again **3 sec/speed 7**.
2. Place a jug on mixing bowl lid. Weigh in water then set jug aside.
3. Add chickpea flour, salt, cumin and turmeric to mixing bowl then, without measuring cup, mix **1 min/speed 3** while slowly adding water through hole in mixing bowl lid. Scrape down sides and base of mixing bowl with spatula. Mix again **10 sec/speed 4**. Transfer to a bowl and leave to rest for 30 minutes. Meanwhile, clean mixing bowl and make filling.

Filling

4. Place oil and cumin seeds in mixing bowl then fry **5 min/Varoma/speed 1**.
5. Add onions and chop **5 sec/speed 7**. Scrape down sides of mixing bowl with spatula then sauté **8 min/120°C/speed**.
6. Add cumin, turmeric, chilli powder and nutmeg then fry **1 min 30 sec/100°C/speed**.
7. Add garlic, paneer and spinach then chop **3 sec/speed 5** while stirring with spatula through hole in mixing bowl lid. Cook **3 min/100°C/speed**. Scrape down sides of mixing bowl with spatula.

Continued on page **106** ▶

25 min

1 hour

easy

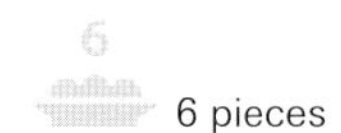
6 pieces

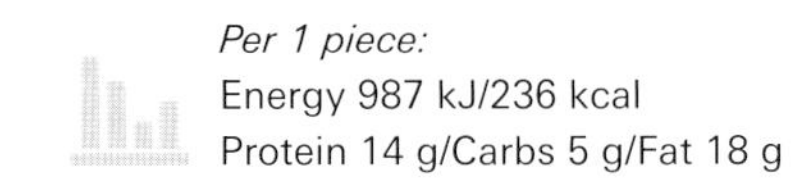
Per 1 piece:
Energy 987 kJ/236 kcal
Protein 14 g/Carbs 5 g/Fat 18 g

▶ PUDLA WITH SPINACH AND PANEER, continued

8. Add cream and salt then simmer **2 min/95°C/speed**.
9. Heat 2 tsp oil in a small non-stick frying pan or pancake pan over a medium heat. Pour a ladleful of pudla batter into pan and spread out a little to form a thick pancake. Cook for 2 minutes until golden then flip over. Cook for a further minute then transfer to a hot plate and keep warm.
10. Repeat until all batter has been used, adding more oil as necessary. Spoon some hot filling into each pancake, fold over and serve warm.

VARIATION

- For a spicy pancake version, add a halved fresh green chilli to batter in step 1.

CHANA MASALA

Arguably the most popular vegetarian dish in India, this combination of hearty, comforting pulses and rich, deeply spiced, tomato-based sauce makes it perfect for anyone. Serve as a vegetarian main, as a side dish as part of a banquet, or as a snack with breads.

INGREDIENTS

- 3 garlic cloves
- 2 fresh green chillies, halved, deseeded if desired
- 25 g fresh root ginger, peeled, cut in round slices (2 mm)
- 15 g vegetable oil
- 100 g onions, quartered
- 2 tsp ground coriander
- 2 tsp ground cumin
- 2 tsp Kashmiri chilli powder
- ½ tsp ground turmeric
- 400 g tinned chopped tomatoes (1 x 400 g tin)
- 600 g cooked chickpeas (drained weight) or 250 g dried chickpeas, soaked overnight, then boiled for 45 minutes until tender
- 300 g water
- 2 tsp fine sea salt
- 1 tsp garam masala
- 1 Tbsp lemon juice
- 1 small handful fresh coriander leaves, chopped, for garnish (approx. 5 g)

PREPARATION

1. Place garlic, chillies and ginger in mixing bowl then chop **3 sec/speed 7**. Scrape down sides of mixing bowl with spatula then chop again **3 sec/speed 7**. Transfer to a bowl and set aside.
2. Place oil and onions in mixing bowl then chop **5 sec/speed 5**. Scrape down sides of mixing bowl with spatula then sauté **10 min/120°C/speed** .
3. Add reserved chopped garlic, chillies and ginger then fry **1 min/100°C/speed 0.5**.
4. Add ground coriander, cumin, chilli powder and turmeric then fry **1 min/100°C/speed 0.5**.
5. Add tomatoes, chickpeas and water then simmer **20 min/98°C/ /speed** .
6. Add salt, garam masala and lemon juice then stir in with spatula. Sprinkle with chopped coriander leaves before serving.

 10 min  45 min  easy  4 portions

Per 1 portion:
Energy 1182 kJ/283 kcal
Protein 14 g/Carbs 34 g/Fat 10 g

TARKA DAL

'Tarka' here refers to the method where spices and chillies are fried and added to the dish at the end of cooking. Like many spiced dishes, you may find this tastes better reheated the day after it's been prepared, when the flavours have had more time to develop. It is a great, economical accompaniment to dry curries and rice to complete a meal. Dal is eaten very widely in India and is a good source of protein.

INGREDIENTS

250 g mung dal
700 g water, plus extra for soaking
6 garlic cloves, finely sliced
1 tsp vegetable oil
1 tsp cumin seeds
40 g ghee
70 g onions, quartered
15 g fresh root ginger, peeled, cut in round slices (2 mm)
1-2 fresh green chillies, halved, deseeded, to taste
½ tsp ground turmeric
2 tsp garam masala
1 tsp fine sea salt, or to taste
1 small handful fresh coriander leaves, chopped, for garnish (approx. 5 g)

USEFUL ITEMS

large bowl

PREPARATION

1. Soak mung dal for at least 8 hours or overnight in plenty of water. Rinse well then drain.
2. Place soaked and drained mung dal, water and 2 finely sliced garlic cloves in mixing bowl. Replace measuring cup with simmering basket, then boil **8 min/100°C/ /speed** . Skim froth from surface and discard.
3. Add oil, then replace measuring cup with simmering basket, and simmer **25 min/98°C/ /speed** . Transfer to a bowl (do not drain) and keep warm. Clean and dry mixing bowl.
4. Place cumin seeds in mixing bowl and toast **5 min/Varoma/speed** .
5. Add ghee, onions, ginger and chillies then chop **5 sec/speed 5**. Scrape down sides of mixing bowl with spatula then sauté **5 min/120°C/speed 0.5**.
6. Add remaining 4 finely sliced garlic cloves, turmeric, garam masala and salt then cook **5 min/100°C/speed 0.5**.
7. Add reserved cooked lentil mixture and stir **30 sec/ /speed 2.5**. Stir in chopped coriander leaves just before serving.

TIP

- If the mixture boils up onto the mixing bowl lid then reduce the cooking temperature to 95°C for 2 minutes before turning up to 98°C again in step 3.

VARIATION

- For a quicker version, use red split lentils which require no soaking.

15 min

9 hour
5 min

easy

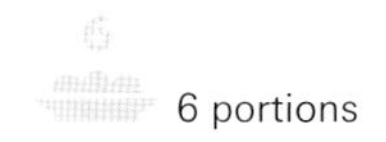
6 portions

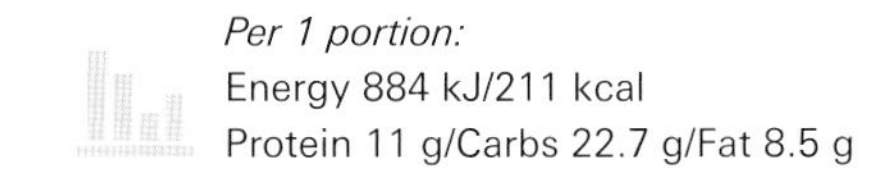
Per 1 portion:
Energy 884 kJ/211 kcal
Protein 11 g/Carbs 22.7 g/Fat 8.5 g

DAL MAKHANI

This black lentil and kidney bean based Punjabi dish is served right across India. It is a rich vegetarian dish that can be served with bread or rice, or alongside other curries as part of a selection. Because of the lengthy total time (due to the soaking of the lentils and beans) this dish needs a bit of planning. It traditionally appears at weddings and parties.

INGREDIENTS

140 g urad beans (black lentils)
40 g kidney beans, dried
600 g water, plus extra for soaking
20 g fresh root ginger, peeled, cut in round slices (2 mm)
1 tsp Kashmiri chilli powder
20 g ghee
2 tsp cumin seeds
70 g onions, quartered
6 garlic cloves
1 tsp fine sea salt
100 g tinned chopped tomatoes
50-70 g double cream, to taste, plus extra for serving
1 tsp garam masala

USEFUL ITEMS

jug
fine sieve

PREPARATION

1. Soak urad and kidney beans for at least 8 hours or overnight in plenty of water. Rinse well twice, ensuring any grit is removed, then drain.
2. Place soaked and drained urad and kidney beans, water, 10 g ginger and chilli powder in mixing bowl then cook **30 min/100°C/⟲/speed 1** until beans are soft. Drain, reserving cooking water and set aside.
3. Place ghee and cumin seeds in mixing bowl then fry **5 min/Varoma/speed** .
4. Add onions and chop **5 sec/speed 5**. Scrape down sides of mixing bowl with spatula then sauté **5 min/120°C/speed 0.5**.
5. Add remaining 10 g ginger, garlic, salt and tomatoes then chop **3 sec/speed 7**. Scrape down sides and lid of mixing bowl with spatula then cook **3 min/100°C/speed 0.5**.
6. Add reserved cooked dal then cook **2 min/100°C/speed 4**.
7. Add 150 g reserved cooking water then simmer **15 min/90°C/speed** .
8. Add cream and garam masala then cook **5 min/90°C/speed** . Serve garnished with a drizzle of cream.

VARIATION

- For a thicker dal, only add 100 g reserved cooking water in step 7.

20 min

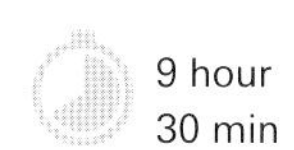
9 hour 30 min

easy

6 portions

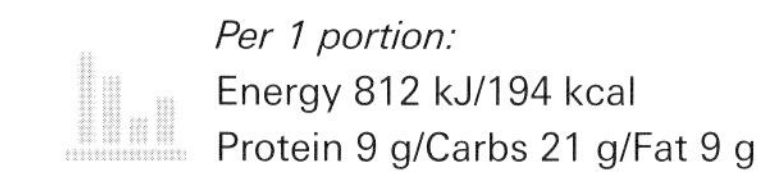
Per 1 portion:
Energy 812 kJ/194 kcal
Protein 9 g/Carbs 21 g/Fat 9 g

PANEER MAKHANI

This popular Punjabi dish has a rich tomato sauce. Blending cashew nuts to form a paste, which is then added to the aromatic sauce, makes it extra creamy. Use paneer made in your Thermomix® (page 28) for a completely homemade version. Serve with Indian bread or over rice.

INGREDIENTS

25 g raw cashew nuts
200 g water, plus 2 Tbsp
5 garlic cloves
20 g fresh root ginger, peeled, cut in round slices (2 mm)
50 g ghee, plus extra for frying
70 g onions, quartered
300 g passata
1½ tsp fine sea salt
1 tsp desiccated coconut
1 tsp Kashmiri chilli powder
½ tsp ground coriander
½ tsp ground cumin
½ tsp ground cinnamon
½ tsp garam masala
¼ tsp ground turmeric
250 g mixed vegetables (e.g. potatoes, carrots, cauliflower, cut in 2 cm pieces, or peas)
250 g paneer cheese, diced (2 cm)
75 g plain yoghurt
50 g double cream
½ tsp caster sugar
1 small handful fresh coriander leaves, chopped, for garnish (approx. 5 g)

USEFUL ITEMS

frying pan

PREPARATION

1. Place cashew nuts and 2 Tbsp water in mixing bowl then blend **30 sec/speed 10**. Transfer to a small bowl and set aside. Rinse mixing bowl.
2. Place garlic and ginger in mixing bowl then grate **5 sec/speed 7**. Scrape down sides of mixing bowl with spatula then grate again **5 sec/speed 7**. Transfer to a small bowl and set aside.
3. Place ghee in mixing bowl and heat **2 min/100°C/speed 1**.
4. Add onions and chop **3 sec/speed 5**. Sauté **5 min/120°C/speed 0.5**.
5. Add reserved grated garlic and ginger then fry **1 min/100°C/speed 0.5**.
6. Add passata and cook **5 min/100°C/speed 1**.
7. Add salt, coconut, chilli powder, ground coriander, cumin, cinnamon, garam masala, turmeric and 100 g water then simmer **10 min/98°C/speed 1**.
8. Add mixed vegetables, remaining 100 g water and reserved cashew paste then simmer **10 min/98°C/⟲/speed 1**. Meanwhile, fry diced paneer in a frying pan with a little ghee, over a medium heat, until golden on all sides. Check vegetables are cooked and prolong cooking if necessary.
9. Add yoghurt, cream, sugar and reserved fried paneer then cook **2 min/98°C/⟲/speed 🥄**. Garnish with chopped coriander leaves before serving.

20 min

1 hour

easy

4 portions

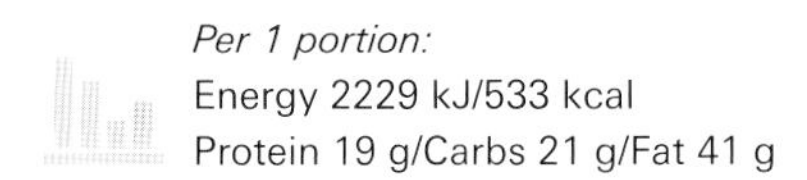
Per 1 portion:
Energy 2229 kJ/533 kcal
Protein 19 g/Carbs 21 g/Fat 41 g

NADAN MUTTA (EGG CURRY)

This is a very popular dish in Kerala where it is often served as breakfast with fermented rice pancakes (dosa). Also known as egg roast, eggs are boiled and served with a fresh onion and tomato sauce that can be fiery or not, should you wish to decrease the chillies. It makes a protein-packed vegetarian main, or a side dish.

INGREDIENTS

30 g coconut oil
1 tsp dried fennel seeds
250 g onions, quartered
20 g fresh root ginger, peeled, cut in round slices (2 mm)
4 garlic cloves
2 dried Kashmiri chillies
1 tsp ground coriander
1 tsp ground cumin
1 tsp Kashmiri chilli powder
1 tsp ground black pepper
½ tsp ground turmeric
400 g passata
1 pinch fine sea salt
6 hard-boiled eggs, peeled
1 small handful fresh coriander leaves, chopped, for garnish (approx. 5 g)

USEFUL ITEMS

cling film
serving bowl

PREPARATION

1. Place coconut oil and fennel seeds in mixing bowl then fry **5 min/100°C/speed** ↺.
2. Add onions and chop **3 sec/speed 5**. Scrape down sides of mixing bowl with spatula then sauté **10 min/120°C/speed** ↺.
3. Add ginger and garlic then chop **3 sec/speed 7**. Scrape down sides of mixing bowl with spatula.
4. Add chillies then fry **3 min/100°C/speed 0.5**.
5. Add ground coriander, cumin, chilli powder, pepper and turmeric then fry **1 min/100°C/speed 0.5**.
6. Add passata and salt then simmer **10 min/98°C/speed 0.5**.
7. Place eggs in a serving bowl and pour over sauce, cover with cling film, then leave to heat through for 5 minutes. Serve garnished with chopped coriander leaves.

15 min

50 min
easy

4 portions
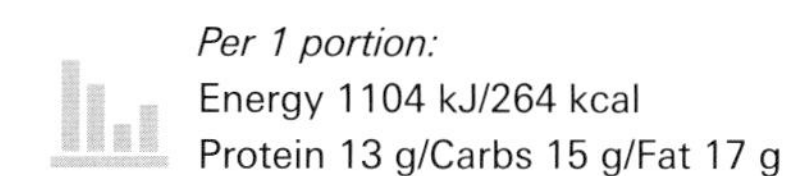
Per 1 portion:
Energy 1104 kJ/264 kcal
Protein 13 g/Carbs 15 g/Fat 17 g

MASALA KADDU (PUMPKIN CURRY)

This wonderfully fiery autumn dish makes it a warming option for colder nights. Yoghurt always helps foil the fiery taste, but also feel free to reduce the chillies.

INGREDIENTS

30 g olive oil
½ tsp onion seeds
2 dried red chillies
300 g onions, quartered
450 g pumpkin flesh, diced (1 cm)
½ tsp ground turmeric
¼-½ tsp chilli powder, to taste
½ tsp fine sea salt
4 Tbsp plain yoghurt, for serving (optional)

PREPARATION

1. Place oil, onion seeds and chillies in mixing bowl then fry **4 min/Varoma/speed** .
2. Add onions and chop **5 sec/speed 5**. Scrape down sides and lid of mixing bowl with spatula then sauté **8 min/120°C/speed** .
3. Add pumpkin, turmeric, chilli powder and salt then cook **5 min/Varoma/ /speed** . Without measuring cup, cook again **10 min/100°C/ /speed** .
4. Serve with yoghurt (if using) as a vegetarian main course or side dish.

10 min

40 min

easy
4 portions
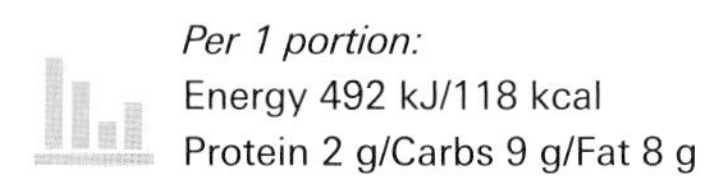
Per 1 portion:
Energy 492 kJ/118 kcal
Protein 2 g/Carbs 9 g/Fat 8 g

VEGETABLE BIRYANI

Biryani, another classic that has many variations, originates from the Moghul influence on Indian cuisine. It is traditionally made with the rice cooking in the steam of the meat or vegetables and it should be light and fluffy. The flavour and results achieved in the Thermomix® are fabulous.

INGREDIENTS

Rice

2 garlic cloves
10 g fresh root ginger, peeled, cut in round slices (2 mm)
50 g ghee
300 g basmati rice, rinsed
1 tsp cumin seeds
2 tsp ground turmeric
½ tsp black mustard seeds
1 Tbsp curry powder

Vegetables

1000 g water
150 g waxy potatoes, peeled, diced (2 cm)
100 g carrots, sliced (1 cm)
150 g frozen green peas
75 g cashew nuts
50 g sultanas

Sauce

100 g plain yoghurt
1 tsp garam masala
½ tsp fine sea salt
1 Tbsp lemon juice

USEFUL ITEMS

cling film
serving bowl
jug

PREPARATION

Rice

1. Place garlic and ginger in mixing bowl then chop **3 sec/speed 8**. Scrape down sides of mixing bowl with spatula.
2. Add ghee and melt **2 min/90°C/speed** .
3. Add rice, cumin seeds, turmeric, mustard seeds and curry powder then heat **3 min/100°C/speed** . Transfer to simmering basket.

Vegetables

4. Place water in mixing bowl and insert simmering basket with contents. Place Varoma dish into position then weigh in potatoes and carrots.
5. Insert Varoma tray and weigh in peas, cashew nuts and sultanas. Cover Varoma and steam **25 min/Varoma/speed 2** until rice and vegetables are cooked. Transfer rice and vegetables to a large serving bowl. Stir then cover with cling film and keep warm.
6. Transfer steaming water to a jug then weigh 100 g steaming liquid back into mixing bowl.

Sauce

7. Add yoghurt, garam masala and salt then mix **10 sec/speed 5.** Pour over rice and vegetables then drizzle with lemon juice. Cover and leave to stand for 5 minutes before serving.

VARIATIONS

- Try using roughly chopped dried figs or dried apricots instead of sultanas.
- Almonds or pistachio nuts would also make a good alternative to cashew nuts.

15 min

50 min

easy

4 portions

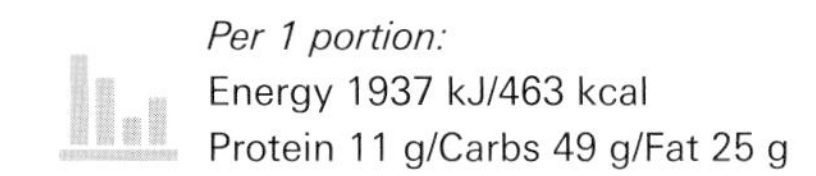
Per 1 portion:
Energy 1937 kJ/463 kcal
Protein 11 g/Carbs 49 g/Fat 25 g

ALOO GOBI (BOMBAY POTATOES WITH CAULIFLOWER)

Potatoes and cauliflower may sound like humble vegetables, but they take on all the flavour and vibrancy of their spice partners in this chunky, dry vegetable curry. This classic everyday dish also makes an excellent accompaniment to your favourite curries – or serve it with an egg on top for breakfast!

INGREDIENTS

2 garlic cloves
500 g water
40 g vegetable oil, plus 1 tsp
500 g waxy Charlotte potatoes, scrubbed, diced (3 cm)
200 g cauliflower florets (3 cm)
1 tsp fine sea salt
1 tsp ground cumin
1½ tsp ground coriander
¼ tsp ground turmeric
¼ tsp chilli powder
2 dried red chillies
200 g tinned tomatoes
½ tsp lemon juice

USEFUL ITEMS

jug
serving dish

PREPARATION

1. Place garlic in mixing bowl and chop **3 sec/speed 8**. Transfer to a bowl and set aside.
2. Place water and 1 tsp oil in mixing bowl. Insert simmering basket and weigh in potatoes. Place Varoma dish into position and weigh in cauliflower florets, cover then steam **14-16 min/Varoma/speed 1** until potatoes are just cooked. Meanwhile, add salt, cumin, coriander, turmeric and chilli powder to chopped garlic. Check potatoes are cooked (see tip).
3. Set Varoma aside and keep warm. Remove simmering basket with aid of spatula then transfer steaming water to a jug and reserve.
4. Place oil and dried chillies in mixing bowl then fry **7 min/120°C/speed 🥄**.
5. Add reserved spices and garlic, tomatoes and 80 g reserved steaming water then cook **5 min/100°C/speed 0.5**.
6. Add reserved steamed potatoes and cauliflower then stir with spatula to coat in sauce. Cook **10 min/100°C/⟲/speed 🥄**.
7. Stir in lemon juice gently with spatula. Transfer to a serving dish and serve hot as a vegetarian main course or side dish.

TIPS

- Different varieties of potato cook at different times. Check potatoes are just cooked in step 2 by inserting a sharp knife, and prolong cooking time if necessary.
- This is a chunky, quite dry, vegetable curry. Waxy potatoes like Charlotte are recommended, and it is best if they are scrubbed but not peeled. Peeling them, cutting them smaller, or using other potato varieties may produce a different result.

15 min

50 min

easy

4 portions
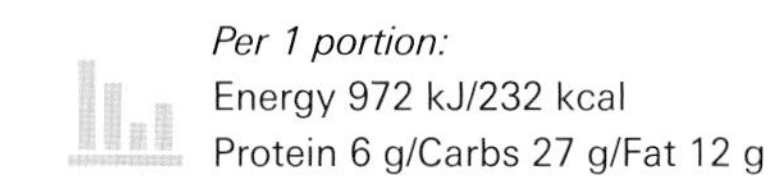
Per 1 portion:
Energy 972 kJ/232 kcal
Protein 6 g/Carbs 27 g/Fat 12 g

ON THE SIDE (PICKLES AND SALADS)

CARROT AND COCONUT SALAD

A zingy and fresh accompaniment to your fiery dishes, this colourful salad is ready in seconds with Thermomix®!

INGREDIENTS

225 g carrots, cut in pieces
40 g onions, cut in pieces
50 g desiccated coconut
15 g lime juice
1 small handful fresh coriander leaves (approx. 5 g)
1 fresh green chilli, halved, deseeded
½ tsp fine sea salt

USEFUL ITEMS

serving bowl

PREPARATION

1. Place carrots, onions, coconut, lime juice, fresh coriander and chilli in mixing bowl then chop **4 sec/speed 5**. Transfer to a serving bowl.
2. Stir in salt just before serving.

 5 min

 5 min

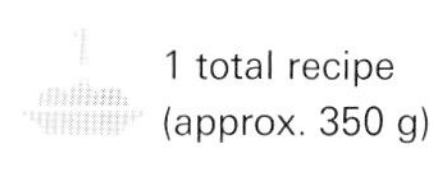 easy

1 total recipe (approx. 350 g)

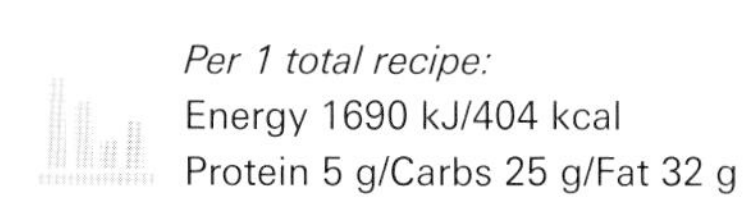

Per 1 total recipe:
Energy 1690 kJ/404 kcal
Protein 5 g/Carbs 25 g/Fat 32 g

ONION RELISH

Another ready in seconds fresh accompaniment. Serve with poppadoms or alongside starters and curries.

INGREDIENTS

220 g onions, quartered
15 g lemon juice
1 fresh green chilli, halved, deseeded
3-6 sprigs fresh mint leaves, to taste
3-6 sprigs fresh coriander leaves, to taste
¼-½ tsp fine sea salt, to taste

USEFUL ITEMS

serving bowl

PREPARATION

1. Place onions, lemon juice, chilli, mint and coriander leaves in mixing bowl then chop **5 sec/speed 6**. Scrape down sides of mixing bowl with spatula then chop again **2 sec/speed 6**. Transfer to a serving bowl.
2. Add salt just before serving.

 5 min

 5 min

 easy

 1 total recipe (approx. 240 g)

Per 1 total recipe:
Energy 364 kJ/87 kcal
Protein 3 g/Carbs 18 g/Fat < 1 g

KACHUMBER (ONION, TOMATO AND CUCUMBER SALAD)

This incredibly easy salad makes a very refreshing, cooling accompaniment to curries and rice dishes.

INGREDIENTS

170 g onions, quartered
2 tsp lime juice or lemon juice
1 tsp white wine vinegar
¼ tsp chilli powder
1 pinch fine sea salt, or to taste
200 g fresh tomatoes, quartered
200 g cucumber, deseeded, cut in pieces (3 cm)

PREPARATION

1. Place onions, lime juice, vinegar, chilli powder and salt in mixing bowl then chop **5 sec/speed 4.5**.
2. Add tomatoes and cucumber then chop **4 sec/speed 4**. Serve immediately.

VARIATION

- Add lettuce, in pieces, in step 2.

 5 min

 5 min

 easy

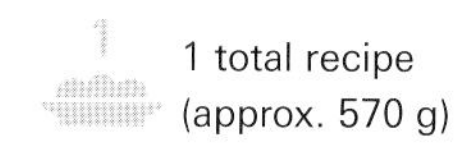
1 total recipe (approx. 570 g)

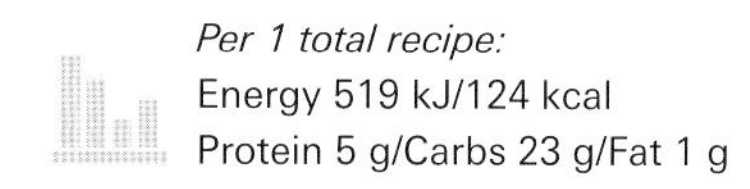
Per 1 total recipe:
Energy 519 kJ/124 kcal
Protein 5 g/Carbs 23 g/Fat 1 g

CORIANDER CHUTNEY

Chutney in an Indian recipe is usually a fresh condiment, unlike a western chutney which is a preserved dish. Coriander, lemon and chilli give this beautifully fresh accompaniment a lovely zing. Serve alongside a variety of curries including chicken tikka (page 56) or aloo gobi (page 120).

INGREDIENTS

60 g onions, quartered
100 g fresh coriander, leaves and stalks
40 g lemon juice
1-2 fresh green chillies, halved, deseeded, to taste
¼ tsp fine sea salt
1 tsp sugar

USEFUL ITEMS

serving bowl
cling film

PREPARATION

1. Place onions, coriander, lemon juice and chillies in mixing bowl then chop **7 sec/speed 7**. Scrape down sides of mixing bowl with spatula then chop again **5 sec/speed 4**.
2. Add salt and sugar then blend **3 sec/speed 8**. Scrape down sides of mixing bowl with spatula then blend again **3 sec/speed 8**. Transfer to a serving bowl, cover with cling film and refrigerate until ready to serve.

5 min  5 min  easy 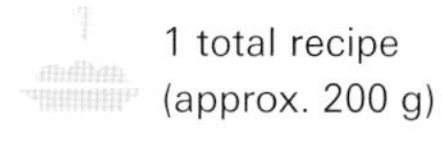 1 total recipe (approx. 200 g)

Per 1 total recipe:
Energy 314 kJ/75 kcal
Protein 3 g/Carbs 14 g/Fat < 1 g

BAINGAN RAITA (AUBERGINE RAITA)

Raita is made by mixing yoghurt with different vegetables (like aubergine here, or cucumber or tomato). It makes a great accompaniment to any Indian food – being particularly useful alongside the more spicy curries! Yoghurt has a cooling effect and it is also good for the digestive system.

INGREDIENTS
300 g plain yoghurt
130 g aubergines, halved then sliced (1 cm)
35 g vegetable oil
½ tsp fine sea salt
½ tsp ground cumin
½ tsp chilli powder

USEFUL ITEMS
serving bowl

PREPARATION
1. Place a serving bowl on mixing bowl lid and weigh in yoghurt then set aside.
2. Place aubergines in mixing bowl and roughly chop **4 sec/speed 4**. Scrape down sides of mixing bowl with spatula.
3. Add oil and fry **10 min/100°C/speed** (symbol). Meanwhile, add salt, cumin and chilli powder to yoghurt in serving bowl then mix well.
4. Transfer aubergines and juice to bowl with spiced yoghurt then stir well. Chill in fridge before serving.

5 min 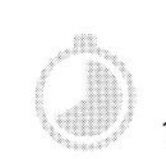 15 min  easy 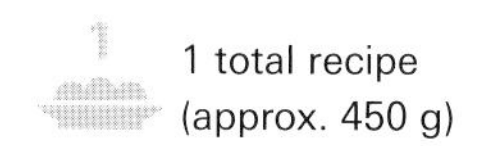 1 total recipe (approx. 450 g) 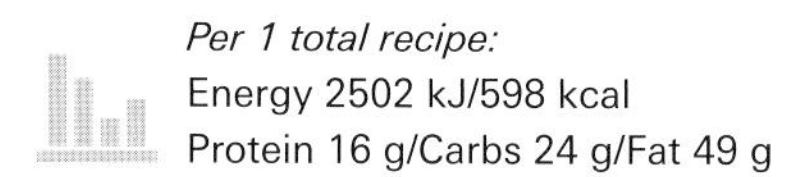

Per 1 total recipe:
Energy 2502 kJ/598 kcal
Protein 16 g/Carbs 24 g/Fat 49 g

SESAME SEED AND TOMATO CHUTNEY

This vibrant chutney is very versatile and can be served alongside starters, main dishes or breads as a dip.

INGREDIENTS

Chutney
30 g sesame seeds
30 g groundnut oil
150 g onions, quartered
½ tsp chilli powder
½ tsp ground turmeric
1 pinch asafoetida
400 g fresh tomatoes, quartered
20 g chana dal (yellow dried split peas), rinsed

Temper
1 Tbsp groundnut oil
½ tsp black mustard seeds
1 fresh red chilli, halved, deseeded, thinly sliced

PREPARATION

Chutney
1. Place sesame seeds in mixing bowl and toast **5 min/Varoma/speed 1.5**. Transfer to a small bowl and set aside.
2. Place oil and onions in mixing bowl then chop **5 sec/speed 5**. Scrape down sides of mixing bowl with spatula then sauté **5 min/120°C/speed** .
3. Add chilli powder, turmeric, asafoetida and reserved toasted sesame seeds then sauté **1 min/100°C/speed** .
4. Add tomatoes and chana dal then cook **12 min/100°C/speed 0.5**. Blend **30 sec/speed 10**. Transfer to a bowl and set aside to cool (approx. 30 minutes).

Temper
5. Once chutney is cool, place oil, mustard seeds and chilli in mixing bowl then fry **5 min/Varoma/speed** .
6. Pour over cooled chutney and serve.

10 min

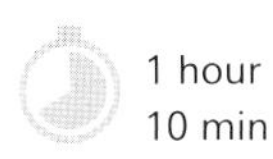
1 hour 10 min

easy

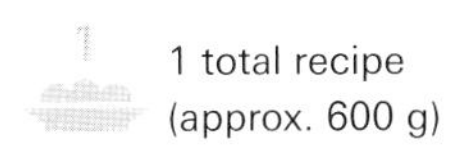
1 total recipe (approx. 600 g)

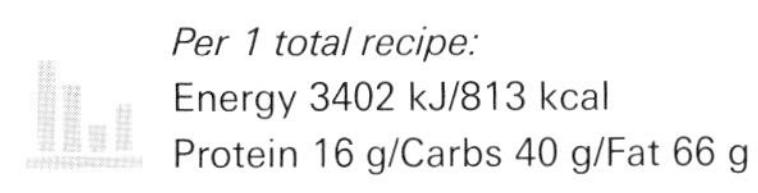
Per 1 total recipe:
Energy 3402 kJ/813 kcal
Protein 16 g/Carbs 40 g/Fat 66 g

BRINJAL PICKLE (AUBERGINE PICKLE)

This unique, sweet aubergine pickle is another accompaniment that goes brilliantly with just about everything. For the best flavour, leave to mature for a few weeks before using.

INGREDIENTS

30 g fresh root ginger, peeled, cut in round slices (2 mm)
1 fresh green chilli, halved, deseeded
2 garlic cloves
2 tsp ground turmeric
2 tsp ground ginger
½ tsp chilli powder
220 g white wine vinegar
1½ tsp cumin seeds
1½ tsp fenugreek seeds
130 g sesame oil
110 g sugar
1 Tbsp fine sea salt
600 g aubergines, diced (2 cm)

USEFUL ITEMS

sterilised jam jars

PREPARATION

1. Place fresh ginger, chilli and garlic in mixing bowl then chop **10 sec/speed 6**. Scrape down sides of mixing bowl with spatula.
2. Add turmeric, ground ginger, chilli powder and 40 g vinegar then mix **10 sec/speed 4**. Transfer to a bowl and set aside.
3. Place cumin, fenugreek and sesame oil in mixing bowl then fry **3 min/Varoma/speed 1**.
4. Add reserved paste and cook **5 min/100°C/speed 1**.
5. Add remaining 180 g vinegar, sugar and salt then mix **10 sec/speed 4**.
6. Add aubergines and cook **20 min/100°C/↺/speed 1**. Pour into warm sterilised jars, seal and label. Allow pickle to mature for 2-3 weeks before serving as a condiment with starters or curries.

TIP

- Once opened, the pickle should be stored in the fridge.

 5 min

 30 min

 easy

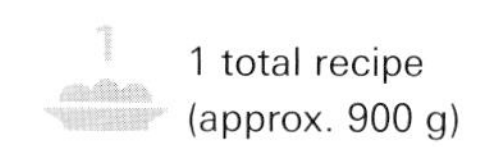 1 total recipe (approx. 900 g)

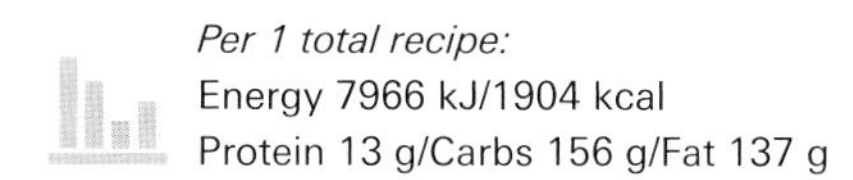

Per 1 total recipe:
Energy 7966 kJ/1904 kcal
Protein 13 g/Carbs 156 g/Fat 137 g

MANGO CHUTNEY

Another classic, this goes with just about everything from poppadoms to your favourite curries, or simply slathered on cold meats and leftovers. Homemade, it contains a far more intense flavour as grinding the spices with sugar in your Thermomix® is a great way to release the oils and aromas. Left to mature for a few weeks before using will only improve the flavour.

INGREDIENTS

1 tsp ground allspice
½ tsp ground ginger
½ tsp ground nutmeg
¼ tsp ground cinnamon
¼ tsp ground cloves
250 g granulated sugar
20 g fresh root ginger, peeled, cut in round slices (2 mm)
1 garlic clove
1 fresh red chilli, halved, deseeded
80 g onions, quartered
150 g light brown sugar
100 g white wine vinegar
¼ tsp fine sea salt
100 g sultanas
350 g ripe mangoes, diced (1 cm)

USEFUL ITEMS

sterilised jam jars

PREPARATION

1. Place allspice, ground ginger, nutmeg, cinnamon, cloves and 100 g granulated sugar in mixing bowl then grind **30 sec/speed 10**.
2. Add fresh ginger, garlic and chilli then chop **5 sec/speed 8**.
3. Add onions and chop **5 sec/speed 5**. Scrape down sides and lid of mixing bowl with spatula.
4. Add remaining 150 g granulated sugar, light brown sugar, vinegar and salt then, replace measuring cup with simmering basket, and cook **30 min/Varoma/speed 3**.
5. Add sultanas and mango then, replace measuring cup with simmering basket, and cook **10 min/100°C/↺/speed ⚲**.
6. Pour into warm sterilised jars, seal and label. Allow chutney to mature for 4 weeks before serving as a condiment to many Indian dishes including curries and starters.

TIP

- Once opened, the chutney should be stored in the fridge.

10 min

50 min

easy

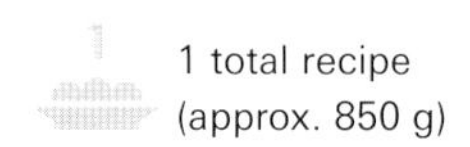

1 total recipe (approx. 850 g)

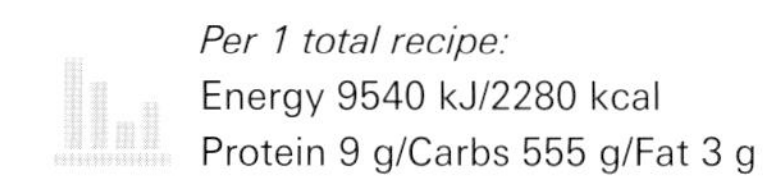

Per 1 total recipe:
Energy 9540 kJ/2280 kcal
Protein 9 g/Carbs 555 g/Fat 3 g

RICE AND BREADS

CUMIN RICE

A simple rice dish lightly spiced with cumin. Adding ingredients during the cooking of the rice enhances the taste of the finished dish. This is made easy with the Thermomix® as the infusion of flavours happens during the steaming process. Also try other ingredients such as lemon peel, onion seeds, cinnamon or curry leaves.

INGREDIENTS

1000 g water
350 g basmati rice (see tip)
2 tsp cumin seeds
1 tsp fine sea salt
1 Tbsp ghee (optional)

USEFUL ITEMS

serving bowl

PREPARATION

1. Place water in mixing bowl. Insert simmering basket and weigh in rice. Stir cumin and salt into rice then rinse rice **10 sec/speed 5**.
2. Steam **20 min/Varoma/speed 4**. Remove simmering basket with aid of spatula and transfer rice to a serving bowl. Stir through ghee (if using) then serve.

TIPS

- Use 50-70 g dry rice per person.
- The maximum amount of dry rice you can cook in the Thermomix® is 350 g.
- If water begins to boil up over the lid, increase blade speed or add 1 tsp oil with water.

VARIATIONS

- For a lower fat version, add ½ Tbsp ghee over rice at step 1 to flavour rice as it cooks, then omit ghee in step 2. Most of the ghee will be left in the steaming water but you will still have a lovely ghee flavour in the rice.
- For a fat-free version, omit ghee completely.

5 min

25 min

easy

6 portions

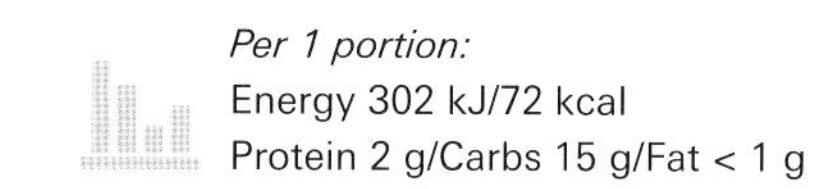

Per 1 portion:
Energy 302 kJ/72 kcal
Protein 2 g/Carbs 15 g/Fat < 1 g

PILAU RICE

An essential part of a curry feast, this is a rice dish that is flavoured and fragrant, adding that special touch to an Indian feast. It is made really easily in your Thermomix®, requiring only a few store cupboard ingredients.

INGREDIENTS

Steamed Basmati Rice

1000 g water
350 g basmati rice (see tip)
1 tsp fine sea salt

Tarka

80 g onions, quartered
25 g ghee
2 cinnamon sticks
6 cardamom pods
1 tsp cumin seeds
1 tsp coriander seeds

USEFUL ITEMS

serving bowl with lid

PREPARATION

Steamed Basmati Rice

1. Place water in mixing bowl. Insert simmering basket and weigh in rice and salt. Rinse rice **10 sec/speed 5** then steam **20 min/Varoma/speed 4**.
2. Remove simmering basket with aid of spatula. Transfer rice to a serving bowl, cover and keep warm. Meanwhile, rinse and dry mixing bowl.

Tarka

3. Place onions in mixing bowl and chop **5 sec/speed 4.5**. Scrape down sides of mixing bowl with spatula.
4. Add ghee, cinnamon, cardamom, cumin and coriander seeds then fry **8 min/Varoma/speed 1**. Pour tarka over rice, mix gently then serve.

TIPS

- Use 50-70 g dry rice per person.
- The maximum amount of dry rice you can cook in the Thermomix® is 350 g.
- If water begins to boil up over the lid, increase blade speed or add 1 tsp oil with water.

10 min

40 min

easy

6 portions

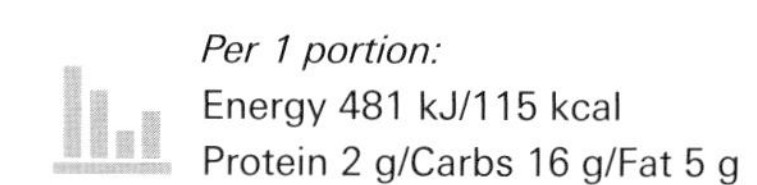

Per 1 portion:
Energy 481 kJ/115 kcal
Protein 2 g/Carbs 16 g/Fat 5 g

CHAPATIS

Chapati or roti is one of the most common staple unleavened breads consumed in India. In Hindi, 'chapat' means 'to slap', and this bread's name originates from the traditional method of forming rounds of dough by slapping the dough between the palms of the hands.

INGREDIENTS

250 g chapati flour, plus extra for dusting
170 g water
10 g vegetable oil, plus extra for greasing
1 tsp fine sea salt

USEFUL ITEMS

cling film
rolling pin
metal spatula
frying pan
tea towel

PREPARATION

1. Place flour in mixing bowl and mix **1 min/speed 10** to heat flour slightly.
2. Add water, oil and salt then knead **4 min/**. Meanwhile, grease a bowl with oil then set aside. Tip dough out onto work surface and bring together into a ball. Place in prepared bowl, cover with cling film and set aside to rest for 30 minutes.
3. Tip rested dough out onto a lightly floured work surface and divide into 15 equal-sized pieces. Using a rolling pin, roll each piece of dough into a circle (Ø 15 cm).
4. Heat a dry frying pan over a high heat. Reduce heat to medium, then cook a chapati for 1-2 minutes until puffed and coloured. Flip over, and using the back of a spatula to press chapati flat, cook for up to 1 minute. Keep chapatis warm in a clean tea towel while cooking remaining pieces of dough. Serve immediately, while still warm.

TIPS

- Chapatis can be reheated by wrapping in foil and placing in a hot oven for 5 minutes.
- Heating the flour in step 1 helps create a soft dough.

Step 4

45 min

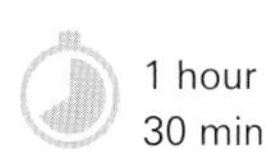
1 hour 30 min

easy

15 pieces

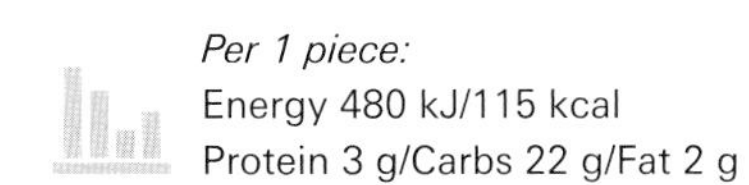
Per 1 piece:
Energy 480 kJ/115 kcal
Protein 3 g/Carbs 22 g/Fat 2 g

STUFFED PARATHAS

These fried flatbreads are slightly denser than oven baked naan breads. They make an excellent accompaniment to curries, either instead of or as well as rice although they're often eaten as breakfast or a teatime snack in India.

INGREDIENTS

Dough

140 g water
300 g chapati flour or bread flour (made up of 150 g white and 150 g wholemeal bread flours)
30 g ghee
15 g vegetable oil, plus extra for greasing
1 tsp fine sea salt

Potato Filling

10 g fresh coriander leaves
50 g onions, halved
1 garlic clove
1-2 fresh green chillies, halved, deseeded if desired, to taste
20 g ghee, plus extra for frying
¼ tsp cumin seeds
1 tsp amchoor (mango powder)
150 g potatoes, peeled, diced (1 cm)
80 g water

USEFUL ITEMS

large bowl
cling film
rolling pin
frying pan
tea towel

PREPARATION

Dough

1. Place water in mixing bowl and heat **1 min 30 sec/37°C/speed 1**.
2. Add flour, ghee, oil and salt then mix **15 sec/speed 4**. Scrape down sides of mixing bowl with spatula then knead **4 min/**. Meanwhile, grease a large bowl with oil then set aside. Tip dough out onto a work surface and bring together into a ball. Place in prepared bowl, cover with cling film and set aside while continuing with recipe.

Potato Filling

3. Clean and dry mixing bowl. Place coriander leaves in mixing bowl and chop **3 sec/speed 8**. Transfer to a small bowl and set aside.
4. Place onions, garlic and chillies in mixing bowl then chop **3 sec/speed 10**. Scrape down sides of mixing bowl with spatula then chop again **3 sec/speed 10**.
5. Avoiding blades, add ghee, cumin seeds and amchoor then cook **3 min/80°C/speed**.
6. Add potatoes and water then cook **20 min/100°C//speed**.
7. Add reserved chopped coriander and mix **10 sec/speed 2**. Transfer to a bowl and set aside to cool for 5 minutes.

Continued on page **146** ▶

45 min

1 hour 20 min

medium

6 pieces

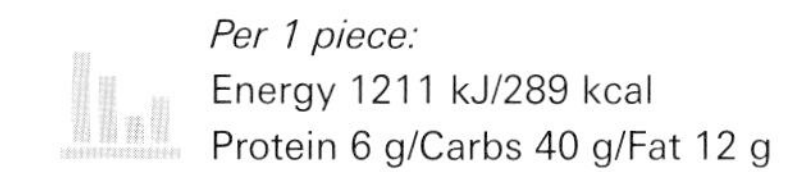
Per 1 piece:
Energy 1211 kJ/289 kcal
Protein 6 g/Carbs 40 g/Fat 12 g

▶ STUFFED PARATHAS, continued

8. Divide rested dough into 6 equal-sized pieces and roll out into circles (Ø 15 cm). Place 2 heaped Tbsp potato mixture in the centre of each circle. Pinch edges of dough to the middle, encasing the filling and press together to form a ball. Carefully and gently, use your fingertips to flatten each circle (approx. Ø 15-18 cm).
9. Heat a frying pan over a medium heat. Fry parathas in a little ghee until golden brown, approx. 3-4 minutes on each side.
10. Keep breads warm in a clean tea towel while cooking remaining parathas, adding extra ghee as required. Serve immediately while still warm.

TIPS

- Parathas are best fresh, so make just before serving.
- Parathas can be frozen and reheated, wrapped in foil, in a moderate oven for 5 minutes.

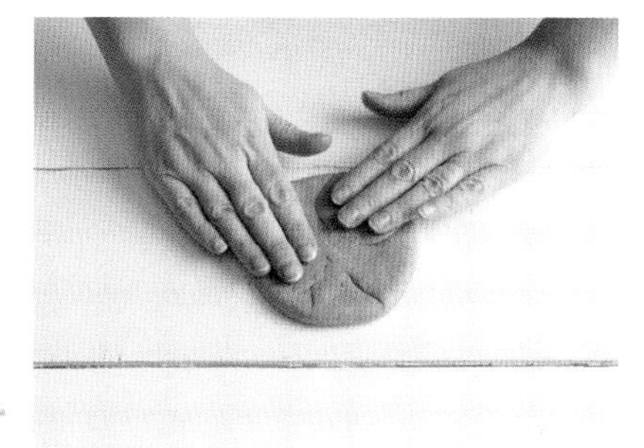

Step 8

PESHWARI NAANS

This sweet variation on the classic flatbread contains an almond, coconut and sultana filling – flavours which provide the perfect balance to spiced dishes. This version has become a firm favourite among our curry houses. Best eaten warm.

INGREDIENTS

Naan Bread
450 g strong white bread flour
200 g plain yoghurt
100 g milk or water, plus extra for sealing
30 g vegetable oil, plus extra for greasing
1 tsp caster sugar
1 tsp fine sea salt
1 tsp dried instant yeast

Peshwari Naan Filling
75 g blanched almonds
25 g desiccated coconut
30 g sultanas
2 Tbsp runny honey, for garnish
2 Tbsp flaked almonds, for garnish

USEFUL ITEMS

cling film
large bowl
rolling pin
baking tray
wire rack

PREPARATION

Naan Bread

1. Place flour, yoghurt, milk, oil, sugar, salt and yeast in mixing bowl then mix **20 sec/speed 3**. Knead **3 min/🌾**. Meanwhile, grease a large bowl with oil. Transfer kneaded dough to prepared bowl. Cover with cling film and leave in a warm place until doubled in size (approx. 1-2 hours). Meanwhile, clean mixing bowl and prepare filling.

Peshwari Naan Filling

2. Place almonds in mixing bowl and grind **15 sec/speed 10**. Scrape down sides of mixing bowl with spatula.
3. Add coconut and sultanas then mix **10 sec/↺/speed 2**. Transfer to a bowl and set aside.
4. Once dough has doubled in size, preheat grill to 220°C and place a baking tray in bottom of grill to heat up.
5. Divide dough into 8 equal-sized pieces then roll out into circles (Ø 15 cm). Place 1½ Tbsp filling over half the dough. Wet edges with a little milk then fold circles in half and seal. Roll out each to a teardrop shape (approx. 18 cm x 10 cm).

Continued on page **148** ▶

 25 min
 2 hour
 medium
 8 pieces
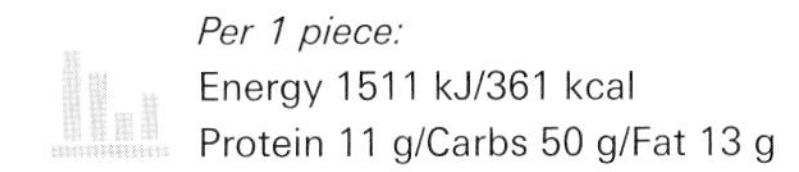
Per 1 piece:
Energy 1511 kJ/361 kcal
Protein 11 g/Carbs 50 g/Fat 13 g

▶ PESHWARI NAANS, continued

6. Place naans on preheated baking tray, in batches if necessary, and grill for 2-3 minutes (220°C) until puffed with brown patches. Turn naans over and grill for a further 2 minutes (220°C) until cooked. Transfer to a wire rack then drizzle honey and scatter flaked almonds over hot naans. Serve immediately, while still warm.

TIP

- Ungarnished naans can be reheated on the same day by sprinkling with a few drops of water and placing in a hot oven for 5 minutes.

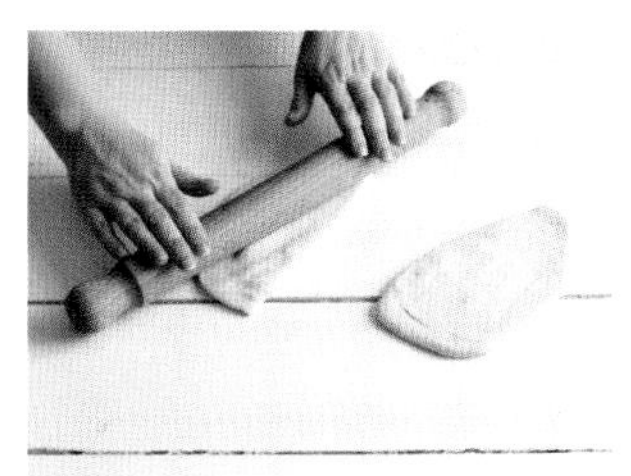

Step 5

NAAN BREAD WITH ONION AND CUMIN

These leavened, oven-baked flatbreads are popular all across Asia. Traditional baking in a clay oven gives them a lovely crunchy exterior with a fluffy inside and a slightly charred appearance – but you can achieve good results in your oven at home. These are Persian in origin, where the word 'naan' translates simply as 'bread'.

INGREDIENTS

1 Tbsp cumin seeds
450 g strong white bread flour, plus extra for dusting
30 g dried onions
200 g plain yoghurt
100 g milk or water
30 g vegetable oil, plus extra for greasing
1 tsp dried instant yeast
1 tsp caster sugar
1 tsp fine sea salt

USEFUL ITEMS

cling film
large bowl
rolling pin
baking tray and paper
tea towel

PREPARATION

1. Place cumin seeds in mixing bowl and toast **3 min/Varoma/speed 1**.
2. Add bread flour, dried onions, yoghurt, milk, oil, yeast, sugar and salt then mix **20 sec/speed 3**.
3. Scrape down sides of mixing bowl with spatula then knead **3 min/**. Meanwhile, grease a large bowl with oil. Transfer kneaded dough to prepared bowl. Cover with cling film and leave in a warm place until doubled in size (approx. 1-2 hours).
4. Towards the end of rising time, preheat oven to 240°C and if you have a separate grill, preheat that as well to 220°C. Line a baking tray with baking paper and place in base of oven to heat up. Meanwhile, on a lightly floured surface, knead dough briefly by hand then divide into 6 equal-sized pieces. Roll each piece into a teardrop shape (approx. 20 cm x 12 cm).
5. Place naans on preheated baking tray, in batches if necessary. Bake for 4-6 minutes (240°C) until puffed and golden.
6. If naans need more browning, either place under hot grill for 30 seconds (220°C), or leave in oven for a further 1 minute (240°C). Wrap in a clean tea towel to keep warm until all naans are baked then serve immediately, while still warm.

TIP

- Naans can be reheated on the same day by sprinkling with a few drops of water and placing in a hot oven for 5 minutes

VARIATION

- For plain naan bread, omit dried onions.

20 min

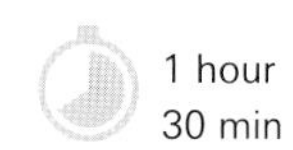
1 hour 30 min

easy

6 pieces

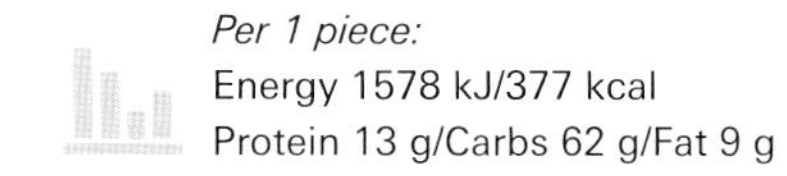
Per 1 piece:
Energy 1578 kJ/377 kcal
Protein 13 g/Carbs 62 g/Fat 9 g

SWEET THINGS AND DRINKS

GULAB JAMUNS

These deliciously rich little cardamom doughnuts are served in a very sweet syrup. They make a comforting end to a spicy meal, and are a common Indian sweet for weddings and banquets.

INGREDIENTS

Syrup
325 g granulated sugar
6 cardamom pods
120 g water

Dough Balls
120 g plain flour
50 g milk powder (whole milk)
2 cardamom pods
1 tsp baking powder
1 pinch saffron threads
30 g butter, diced
70 g plain yoghurt
30 g water
vegetable oil, for frying
20 g flaked almonds, for garnish

USEFUL ITEMS
cling film
deep bowl
deep saucepan or deep fat fryer
slotted spoon
paper towel
saucepan

PREPARATION

Syrup
1. Place sugar and cardamom pods in mixing bowl then grind **30 sec/speed 10**. Scrape down sides of mixing bowl with spatula.
2. Add water and cook **12 min/100°C/speed 2** then cook again **2 min/Varoma/speed 3**. Transfer to a deep bowl, cover with cling film to keep warm then set aside. Meanwhile, make dough balls.

Dough Balls
3. Place flour, whole milk powder, cardamom pods, baking powder and saffron threads in mixing bowl then grind **30 sec/speed 10**. Scrape down sides of mixing bowl with spatula.
4. Add butter, yoghurt and water then knead **20 sec/🌾**. Scrape down sides of mixing bowl with spatula then knead again **10 sec/🌾**.
5. Preheat oil in a deep fat fryer or deep, heavy based saucepan to 170°C. Meanwhile, roll dough mixture into 14 balls (Ø 3 cm).
6. Deep fry balls for 4-6 minutes (170°C) until golden brown and cooked through. Remove with a slotted spoon and drain on paper towel.
7. Add drained balls to bowl with hot syrup and gently stir so all balls are coated. Leave to soak for 1-2 hours (see tip).
8. Reheat dough balls and syrup in a saucepan before serving, garnished with flaked almonds.

TIP
- The flavour of the dough balls is even better if you can leave the balls to infuse in the syrup overnight.

VARIATION
- 1 tsp rose water can also be added to syrup ingredients for a floral note.

25 min

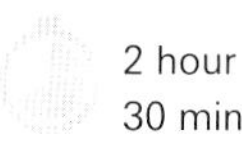
2 hour
30 min

medium

14 pieces

Per 1 piece:
Energy 841 kJ/201 kcal
Protein 2 g/Carbs 33 g/Fat 7 g

LYCHEE PANNA COTTA WITH ROSEWATER SYRUP

Lychees are grown extensively in China, India and the rest of southeast Asia. We have put a fruity Asian twist on the Italian classic of panna cotta to make this delicately flavoured and aromatic dessert.

INGREDIENTS

Lychee Panna Cotta
425 g tinned lychees in syrup, pitted (drained weight 180 g)
500 g double cream
250 g whole milk
80 g granulated sugar
4 gelatine leaves, soaked in cold water for 5 minutes

Rose Water Syrup
80 g caster sugar
2 tsp rose water
1-2 drops pink food colouring (optional)
2 tsp dried rose petals

USEFUL ITEMS
fine sieve
6 individual moulds
jug

PREPARATION

Lychee Panna Cotta
1. Drain lychees through a sieve into a bowl, reserving syrup. Place lychees in mixing bowl and blend **30 sec/speed 8.** Scrape down sides and lid of mixing bowl with spatula then blend again **30 sec/speed 8**. Strain through a fine sieve, collecting purée below. Discard contents of sieve, then set purée aside.
2. Place cream, milk and granulated sugar in mixing bowl then heat **10 min/80°C/speed 3**.
3. Squeeze excess water from soaked gelatine leaves and add to milk.
4. Add 90 g reserved lychee purée and mix **1 min/speed 3**. Pour into 6 individual moulds and allow to cool before chilling in fridge for at least 4 hours, or until set. Meanwhile, clean mixing bowl and make rose water syrup.

Rose Water Syrup
5. Place sugar and 100 g reserved lychee syrup in mixing bowl then heat **4 min/90°C/speed 2**.
6. Add rose water and food colouring (if using) then mix **30 sec/speed 2**. Pour into a jug and set aside to cool.
7. Once panna cottas are set, dip moulds in warm water (5-10 seconds) to loosen, then invert onto plates. Drizzle cooled rose water syrup over the top before serving chilled, garnished with rose petals.

TIP
- Different moulds can be used depending on what you have available. Use silicone moulds, ramekins or dariole moulds. Can also be set and then served in decorative bowls or glasses.

VARIATION
- For a vegetarian option use authentic china grass (agar agar) instead of gelatine to set the dessert.

20 min

4 hour 30 min

easy

6 portions

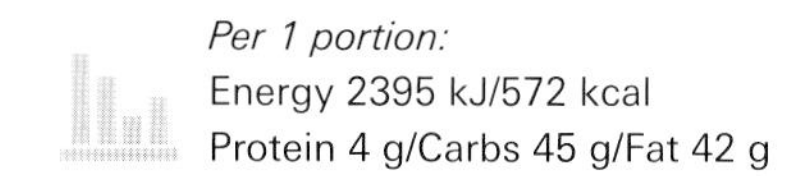
Per 1 portion:
Energy 2395 kJ/572 kcal
Protein 4 g/Carbs 45 g/Fat 42 g

CARDAMOM BREAD AND BUTTER PUDDING

Sometimes you just want a dessert that's hearty and warming, which makes this one an excellent option. It has a lovely crunchy topping, and is wonderful served with vanilla or spice-infused custard.

INGREDIENTS

40 g pistachio nuts, unsalted, peeled
40 g sultanas
350 g whole milk
60 g caster sugar
1 tsp ground cardamom
50 g butter, soft, plus extra for greasing
350 g sliced white bread (approx. 6-7 slices)
150 g double cream
3 large eggs

USEFUL ITEMS

baking dish (approx. 22 cm x 30 cm)

PREPARATION

1. Place pistachios in mixing bowl and chop **2 sec/speed 6**. Transfer to a small bowl.
2. Place small bowl on mixing bowl lid and weigh in sultanas. Set bowl aside.
3. Place milk, sugar and ground cardamom in mixing bowl then heat **5 min/80°C/speed 2**. Meanwhile, grease a baking dish (approx. 22 cm x 30 cm) and spread butter on bread then cut in half diagonally, creating triangles.
4. Arrange bread in overlapping layers in greased baking dish, scattering reserved sultanas and chopped pistachios between layers of bread.
5. Add cream and eggs to infused milk then heat **2 min/80°C/speed 2**. Pour over bread in dish, pressing down to ensure all bread is coated in egg mixture, then leave to soak for 10 minutes. Meanwhile, preheat oven to 180°C.
6. Bake for 25-30 minutes (180°C) until custard is set and top is crunchy. Serve warm.

VARIATION

- Use different dried fruits such as roughly chopped apricots or mixed fruit pieces instead of sultanas.

 15 min

 1 hour

 easy

 6 portions

Per 1 portion:
Energy 2070 kJ/495 kcal
Protein 13 g/Carbs 46 g/Fat 29 g

KHEER WITH DARK CHOCOLATE TOPPING

Kheer is a milk-based pudding made with rice or sometimes vermicelli. It is regularly prepared for festivals, and is an essential part of many Hindu celebrations. Here we use rice and have given it a twist with mandarin flavours and a chocolate topping. It can be served warm if preferred.

INGREDIENTS

Kheer

500 g whole milk
70 g basmati rice, soaked in warm water for 1 hour, then rinsed thoroughly
100 g granulated sugar
½ tsp ground cardamom
50 g mandarin segments, roughly chopped

Dark Chocolate Topping

75 g dark chocolate, 70% cocoa, small pieces or callets
10 g granulated sugar
250 g milk
10 g cornflour
1 medium egg
10 g butter

USEFUL ITEMS

greaseproof paper
6 ramekins or individual dishes

PREPARATION

Kheer

1. Place milk in mixing bowl then, replace measuring cup with simmering basket, and bring to the boil **8 min/100°C/speed 4**.
2. Add soaked and rinsed rice, sugar and ground cardamom then, replace measuring cup with simmering basket, and cook **14 min/98°C/⟲/speed 1**. Transfer to a bowl.
3. Place bowl with rice mixture on mixing bowl lid and weigh in mandarin pieces. Remove bowl then stir. Cool to room temperature then chill completely in fridge. Meanwhile, clean mixing bowl and make topping.

Dark Chocolate Topping

4. Place chocolate and sugar in mixing bowl then grate **10 sec/speed 10**. Scrape down sides of mixing bowl with spatula.
5. Add milk, cornflour and egg then cook **10 min/90°C/speed 3**.
6. Add butter and stir **10 sec/speed 4**. Transfer to a bowl and cover surface with damp greaseproof paper to prevent a skin forming. Once cooled, place in fridge.
7. To serve, divide chilled kheer between 6 ramekins or individual serving dishes, then place a large spoonful of cooled chocolate topping on each.

VARIATION

- Add flaked almonds and/or sultanas to the kheer towards the end of cooking.

10 min

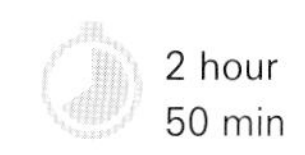
2 hour 50 min

easy

6 portions

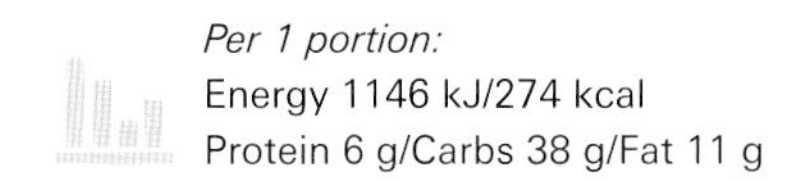
Per 1 portion:
Energy 1146 kJ/274 kcal
Protein 6 g/Carbs 38 g/Fat 11 g

EARL GREY KULFI

Kulfi was made for the Moghul emperors centuries ago. Traditionally it is made by boiling milk to thicken it and flavoured with saffron and/or nuts but nowadays there are many different options available. The hints of Earl Grey in this variation add a floral note to the creamy sweetness.

INGREDIENTS

25 g flaked almonds, toasted
500 g evaporated milk
100 g condensed milk
3 Earl Grey teabags
50 g caster sugar

USEFUL ITEMS

6 kulfi or dariole moulds

PREPARATION

1. Place almonds in mixing bowl and chop **2 sec/speed 4**. Transfer to a bowl and set aside.
2. Place evaporated milk, condensed milk and teabags in mixing bowl then heat **20 min/90°C/⟲/speed ⟡**. Remove teabags and discard.
3. Add sugar and cook **5 min/90°C/speed 3.** Divide between 6 kulfi or dariole moulds and place in freezer until solid (approx. 8 hours).
4. Remove from freezer and unmould (see tip). Serve immediately, decorated with reserved toasted chopped almonds.

TIP

- To unmould, dip the bases in hot water for 5 seconds. Use a knife, if necessary, to ease the kulfi out.

 5 min

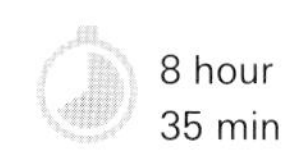 8 hour 35 min

 easy

 6 portions

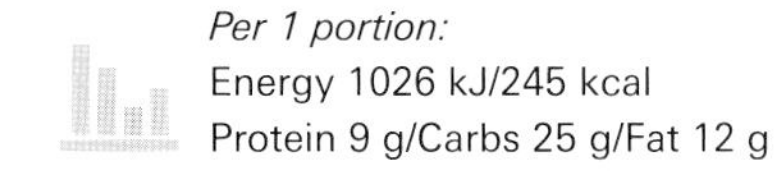
Per 1 portion:
Energy 1026 kJ/245 kcal
Protein 9 g/Carbs 25 g/Fat 12 g

MASALA CHERRY TIFFIN

Although 'tiffin' has now become strongly associated with the British practice of teatime treats, like the chocolate-based refrigerator cake, it is actually an Indian-English word for a light snack. In this recipe it is both – a slightly spiced, chilled, mouth-watering chocolate snack which can be enjoyed with masala chai or coffee!

INGREDIENTS

3 chai teabags
50 g desiccated coconut
150 g glacé cherries
200 g water, boiling
50 g crystallised ginger, in pieces
100 g dried apricots
150 g digestive biscuits, quartered
200 g dark chocolate, 70% cocoa, small pieces or callets
50 g golden syrup
50 g pecan nuts

USEFUL ITEMS

square baking tin (20 cm)
baking paper
large bowl

PREPARATION

1. Line a square baking tin (20 cm) with baking paper.
2. Place teabags in a large bowl then place bowl on mixing bowl lid. Weigh in coconut, cherries and boiling water. Remove bowl and gently mix together with spatula then set aside.
3. Place ginger and apricots in mixing bowl then chop **5 sec/speed 5**. Transfer to bowl with tea.
4. Place biscuits in mixing bowl and crush **3 sec/speed 4**. Transfer to a separate bowl and set aside.
5. Place chocolate and golden syrup in mixing bowl then melt **5 min/50°C/speed** . Scrape down sides of mixing bowl with spatula then melt again **5 min/50°C/speed** . Remove tea bags from large bowl and discard.
6. Add pecan nuts, reserved crushed biscuits and reserved tea-soaked mixture then stir **20 sec/⟲/speed 2**. Spoon into prepared tin and level surface then place in fridge for at least 2 hours or until set.
7. Cut into squares and serve with chai tea.

20 min

2 hour 30 min

easy

12 portions

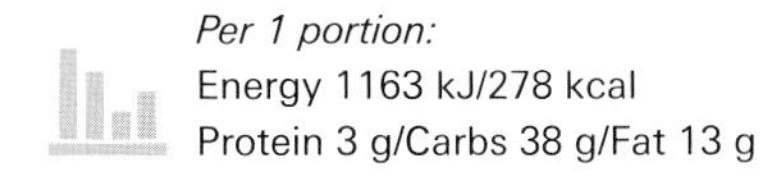
Per 1 portion:
Energy 1163 kJ/278 kcal
Protein 3 g/Carbs 38 g/Fat 13 g

CARDAMOM AND ROSE SHORTBREAD

We've taken a classic British biscuit here and delicately flavoured it with some quintessentially Indian flavours. Lovely served with masala chai or coffee at the end of a meal.

INGREDIENTS

½ tsp ground cardamom
2 tsp dried rose petals
55 g golden caster sugar
40 g long grain rice
100 g ghee
150 g plain flour, plus extra for dusting
1 pinch fine sea salt
2 Tbsp water

USEFUL ITEMS

cling film
baking tray and paper
biscuit cutter (approx. 9 cm x 4 cm)
rolling pin
wire rack
airtight container

PREPARATION

1. Place ground cardamom, rose petals and sugar in mixing bowl then grind **20 sec/speed 10**. Transfer to a bowl and set aside.
2. Place rice in mixing bowl and grind **1 min/speed 10**. Transfer to bowl with sugar and set aside.
3. Place ghee in mixing bowl and whip **20 sec/speed 3**.
4. Add flour, salt and reserved ground sugar and rice then mix **30 sec/speed 4**. Scrape down sides of mixing bowl with spatula.
5. Add water and mix **20 sec/speed 4.** Tip out onto a work surface, wrap in cling film and refrigerate for 45 minutes to firm up. Meanwhile, line a baking tray with baking paper and set aside.
6. Preheat oven to 150°C. Roll out rested dough on a floured surface until 5 mm thick. Cut out biscuits using a biscuit cutter (approx. 9 cm x 4 cm), and place on prepared baking tray. Re-roll any trimmings until all dough is used.
7. Bake for 25-35 minutes (150°C) until cooked through and lightly golden. Transfer to a wire rack to cool and harden. Enjoy straight away or store in an airtight container for up to 5 days.

15 min

1 hour 30 min

easy

12 pieces

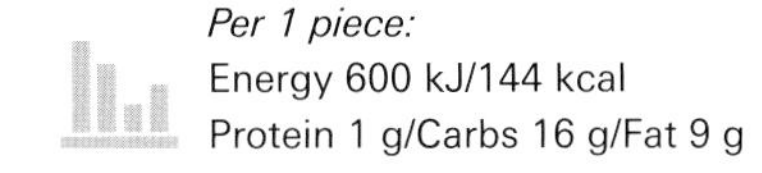
Per 1 piece:
Energy 600 kJ/144 kcal
Protein 1 g/Carbs 16 g/Fat 9 g

MANGO LASSI

Ripe mango can be incredibly sweet and is very much in abundance on the subcontinent making mango lassi a very popular drink. It is delicious and filling, and the sugar can be altered according to personal taste.

INGREDIENTS

400 g ripe mangoes, cut in pieces
600 g plain yoghurt
400 g milk
100 g caster sugar

USEFUL ITEMS

jug

PREPARATION

1. Place mangoes, yoghurt, milk and sugar in mixing bowl then blend **1 min/speed 10**. Transfer to a jug and refrigerate. Serve chilled.

VARIATION

- The amount of sugar can be decreased to as little as 10 g if preferred.

5 min

5 min

easy

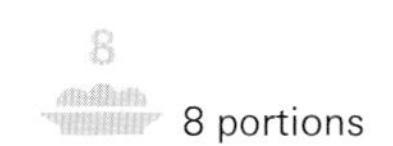
8 portions

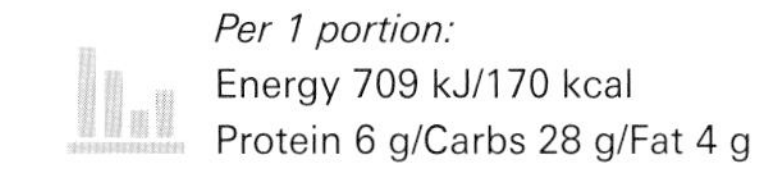
Per 1 portion:
Energy 709 kJ/170 kcal
Protein 6 g/Carbs 28 g/Fat 4 g

STRAWBERRY LASSI

Lassi is a yoghurt-based drink that can be sweet or savoury and modern versions (widely available in restaurants) use fruit as a sweetener. We've teamed it here with a very British fruit. If you're making this in the summer when strawberries are in season and that bit sweeter, you may like to reduce the sugar or omit it completely.

INGREDIENTS

500 g strawberries, hulled
50 g caster sugar
½ tsp ground cardamom
250 g plain yoghurt
100 g ice cubes

USEFUL ITEMS

4 glasses

PREPARATION

1. Place strawberries, sugar and ground cardamom in mixing bowl then blend **30 sec/speed 7**.
2. Add yoghurt and ice then mix **1 min/speed 5**. Pour into glasses and serve immediately.

TIP

- To grind your own cardamom, place a minimum of 2 Tbsp pods in mixing bowl and mix **5 sec/↺/speed 4-6** then discard the husks. Grind the seeds at **speed 10** until fine. Transfer to a sterilised jar and use when needed.

VARIATIONS

- Fresh mint can be substituted for ground cardamom.
- Frozen strawberries can also be used. Omit ice cubes and add water until desired consistency is achieved.

5 min  5 min  easy  4 portions

Per 1 portion:
Energy 587 kJ/140 kcal
Protein 4 g/Carbs 25 g/Fat 3 g

MASALA CHAI

One of the most popular drinks in India, masala chai is a refreshing drink made by brewing black tea with a mixture of aromatic Indian spices and milk. The spices used vary from family to family but include some or all of cardamom, ginger, cinnamon, cloves and pepper. It is commonly referred to only by the word 'chai' and is so easy to make in your Thermomix®. It is great for aiding digestion, too.

INGREDIENTS

1 cardamom pod
3 cloves
1 cinnamon stick
4 black peppercorns
700 g water
500 g milk
20 g caster sugar
5 teabags (e.g. Darjeeling, Ceylon or English Breakfast)
5 g fresh root ginger, peeled, cut in round slices (2 mm)

USEFUL ITEMS

fine mesh sieve

PREPARATION

1. Place cardamom pod, cloves, cinnamon stick and peppercorns in mixing bowl then grind **10 sec/speed 7**.
2. Add water, milk and sugar then insert simmering basket.
3. Place teabags and ginger in simmering basket then heat **12 min/90°C/speed 3**.
4. Remove simmering basket with aid of spatula then strain chai through a fine mesh sieve. Serve immediately while still hot.

5 min

15 min

easy

6 portions

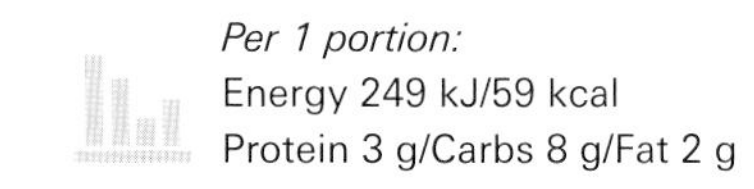
Per 1 portion:
Energy 249 kJ/59 kcal
Protein 3 g/Carbs 8 g/Fat 2 g

GLOSSARY

A

Amchoor
A powder made from dried, unripe green mangoes. It adds a citrusy tang or sourness to foods, as an alternative to vinegar or lemon juice.

Asafoetida
A pungent spice extracted from a fennel-related plant. The strong smell mellows during cooking producing a flavour similar to onion and garlic. Allegedly good for digestion!

Cardamom
Cardamom pods come in two colours and contain small seeds. Green cardamom have a unique spicy-sweet flavour; black cardamom have a stronger, smoky flavour. Pods are often added whole to flavour a dish. Ground cardamom, formed from grinding the seeds, exists as a separate spice.

Chana dal
A split dried pulse, yellow in colour, originating from black chickpeas (kala chana). They will hold their shape during cooking.

Chapati flour
A durum wheat flour that is ground very finely. It is wholegrain and suitable for breads that require no rising.

Dal (Dahl)
A pulse (pea, lentil or bean) that has been split. Also the name of a thick stew made with split pulses e.g. dal makhani.

Dried onions
Onions are sliced and fried until brown and crisp, then dried to preserve their shelf life. Gives a smoky, sweet flavour to dishes as well as adding texture.

F

Fenugreek
Used in Indian cuisine as a herb (fresh or dried leaves – often sold as methi) or a spice (seeds). The leaves have a strong aroma, while the small, hard yellow seeds have a tangy more bitter flavour.

Garam masala
A blend of ground spices that is very common in India, and varies regionally. Spices are toasted then ground producing an aromatic spice blend that forms the base of many Indian dishes.

Garlic powder
Ground dehydrated garlic. A frequently used seasoning in India and a common component of spice mixes.

Ghee
Indian clarified butter (a butter from which water and milk solids have been removed). It has a higher burning point than regular butter making it ideal for frying, as well as a longer shelf life.

Gram flour (Chickpea flour)
A flour made from ground chickpeas that is a staple ingredient in Indian cuisine. It is high in carbohydrates and protein but contains no gluten.

Kashmiri chillies
A smaller, less pungent variety of chilli. Used to give a mild heat and vibrant red colour to dishes.

L

Lassi
A sweet or savoury blend of yoghurt, water, spices and/or fruit. Traditionally salted but modern variations contain fruit. In India they are mostly taken with lunch as a chilled accompaniment.

Lychees
A tropical fruit native to China but grown extensively in India. Encased in a thin shell, the soft white flesh surrounds a large inedible stone, and has a floral, sweet flavour.

M

Masala
Indian term for a blend of spices. There are many versions, an example being garam masala.

Mung dal (Moong dal)
Split and dried green mung beans, without their skins. Yellow in colour, giving tarka dal its traditional appearance.

Mustard seeds
Small round seeds of the mustard plant – can be yellow or black. Used for centuries in Indian cooking, black mustard seeds are more pungent and often used to season dishes as a temper.

Paneer
Fresh, unsalted white cheese. With a dense, crumbly texture and mild flavour, it works well with strong, spicy sauces.

T

Tempering
A method widely used in Indian cuisine whereby spices are heated in hot oil or ghee, and then added to a dish. The hot fat retains the flavour of the spices and carries it into the dish. Can be done at the beginning or end of a recipe.

Tamarind
Tamarind trees yield pods which contain seeds surrounded by a pulp. This is dried and compressed into blocks, or turned into a paste. Adds a subtle sour flavour to curries.

Toor dal
Indian split pigeon peas, which have been a major protein-source for centuries in India.

Urad (Urid) beans/dal
Urad beans are sold as black lentils. When split, the interior is white and they become known as urad dal.

ALPHABETICAL INDEX

A

B

C

🌿 vegetarian *(var.) = variation*

D

E

F

G

H

J

K

L

M

N

O

P

Q

R

S

❦ vegetarian *(var.) = variation*

T

V

X

THANKS

We have lived and breathed India during the past year, and what a pleasure it has been!

With a country as varied as India the challenge for us was to provide an overview that represented this diversity. What we realised is that there was a common thread that ran throughout all the regional cuisines and that was the importance of home cooking. Thermomix® enables us to easily bring a cuisine full of flavour, aroma, colour and spice into our own homes.

Special thanks need to go to Neil Lach-Szyrma who led the majority of the recipe selection and writing process. His passion and enthusiasm for Indian cuisine has infected us all. We hope that with this book we can pass that on to all of you too.

Caroline Snook
Recipe Development Manager

ACKNOWLEDGEMENTS AND COPYRIGHT

Project Manager
Caroline Snook

Recipe development, editing and coordination
Caroline Snook, Neil Lach-Szyrma, Naomi Hutchinson, Katie Chamberlain

Marketing Manager
Sonja Gaydies

Recipe Marketer
Emma Plater

Nutritional values
Rebecca Dandy

Cookbook production
Effizienta, Munich, Germany

Photographer
Cristian Barnett

Food Styling
Mima Sinclair

Prop Styling
Tamzin Ferdinando

Printing
Mohn Media, Germany

With general thanks to:
Rosie Laljee (research and background), recipe testing panel

Edition/Publishing
1st Edition, 2016

www.thermomix.co.uk
www.thermomix.ie